This is the earliest photograph I can find of me, practicing
my kicks in my Mum and Dad's back garden, aged about 12.

To Dave.

I hope you enjoy
Controlled Indignation
and I trust it will
make you smile. Steve

Stay Safe my friend

Dedication

To those who had the courage to
allow the last guardian of their heart
to lower its shield, and allow their
passion for love and life grow to be
an ocean upon which their ship of
dreams sets sail.

For they and they alone truly
understand that having too much
passion can never be enough and that
it would be reckless to underestimate
its power.

Contents

"It's freezing up here.
What do you use to keep warm?"
"Indignation"
replied Michelangelo.
"Best fuel I know...
it never burns out."

'The Agony and the Ecstasy' - by Irving Stone

Controlled Indignation

Indignation is a noun used to describe annoyance provoked by what is perceived as unfair or unjust treatment.

You can be - irate, annoyed, cross, vexed, irritated, exasperated, aggrieved, irked, displeased, provoked, galled, resentful, furious, enraged, infuriated, incensed, raging, maddened, incandescent, wrathful, fuming, ranting, raving, seething, frenzied, beside oneself, outraged and angry.

Anyone can be angry, however, having the right motive to get angry with the right person, at the right time, in the right place, to the right degree... well, that's a lot more difficult. In my experience I have found anger to be a useful tool, but only if I can keep it under control. You can be indignant without being angry and if you are in a state of controlled indignation you will know how to exert minimal effort to achieve maximum impact, while maintaining a focus. Therefore, in my opinion, as far as self-defence is concerned 'indignation' is a much more appropriate word and a far more appropriate and powerful state of mind.

Uncontrolled anger can be your worst enemy and a gift to an experienced opponent. This is because giving in to a bout of furious anger will undoubtedly give you the adrenaline dump and motivation to fight, but sadly, at the same time, would probably leave you wide open for an experienced fighter to take advantage of your rage, which could end badly. If you can avoid it, never strike out of anger as it often strengthens your opponents resolve.

Controlled indignation always leads to positive action. I find that focused and controlled indignation is more effective for combat. It can create the sensation that you are not only in the moment, but that time has slowed down, giving you a sense of control. If, however, uncontrolled anger takes over, things move a lot faster, get out of control and become shambolic very rapidly.

Discipline yourself, because the first person to defeat you could be you. Remember, you are only in control when you are in control of yourself.

Is it true that you cannot win a fight without being really angry? No!

But remember, indignation is an energy that never burns out.

It's 1956 and I'm just a little kid in short pants with skinned knees and a mop of tousled hair. I climbed trees, rolled in the autumn leaves, skipped down the road and ran against the wind in the firm belief that I was the Lone Ranger or on a good day Zorro. Like all children I had neither a past nor a future; I just revelled the present and lived in the moment, which sadly very few of us do as adults.

As Dr. Seuss said "Adults are just obsolete children and the hell with them."…How true is that?

My Dad designed aircraft and had a brain the size of a planet, but Neville my best mate, well his Dad was a bus driver in the City of Manchester, which of course was a far more exciting job, as far as I was concerned.

One day the boss of the bus depot had decided that all the bus conductors needed to learn self-defence and Nev's Dad said they were also going to do a class for kids and he had signed us both up. I remember that Neville protested and did not want to go, but of course I was the Lone Ranger and by definition always up for a fight.

So in the summer of 1956 I was introduced to the art of jujutsu, which marked the beginning of my lifelong love for the martial arts. Mind you, there are occasions when I still think I'm the Lone Ranger or Zorro, and if capes ever come back in to fashion, well I need say no more.

From the first session in that cold damp bus depot I was hooked and from this early age the profound thoughts and skills of the ancient masters fascinated me, so much so that even now some sixty years on the study of ancient and modern combat systems is a passion with me.

Over the years I have had the privilege of training with, and under, some of the world's most eminent authorities in martial arts, self-defence and personal protection as well as the more militaristic close-quarter combat systems used by law enforcement professionals and special forces.

The weird thing is that like my Dad I became a professional designer and writer. In 1986 I established my own business, (PS5) which is now an internationally recognised specialist security consultancy, providing training and educational material to the law enforcement, defence and the security sectors.

The company's training wing 'R.E.A.C.T' delivers highly specialised training protocols to both the private and public sectors with specific focus on weapons related crime and personal protection from violence, aggressive behaviour and terrorism, and I'd like to take this opportunity to thank Neville's dad.

Peering over my 70 year old shoulder is a 10 year old kid (I don't think I've changed a bit).

the learning

The little kid that started this journey is still, I'm pleased to say, by my side and in my head. But, I must say, if I'd known then what I know now I would probably have had a completely different life.

Together, that little boy and I have, for more than 60 years, studied, practiced and taught Martial arts & Self Defence, and in my later years have written many books and editorial features. During those years I have acquired skills that enable me to inflict physical pain on others. However, when it comes to inflicting pain, I have concluded that it comes down to a simple common denominator… 'Truth'

Do I always tell the truth? .... ***NO!***
Am I always honest? .... ***NO!***
Do I always say what I feel? .... ***NO!***
Am I a liar? .... ***NO!***

And why?...

Because, although I know blatant lying is destructive and harmful, I also know that telling the absolute truth, saying what I feel and being totally honest can sometimes hurt even more, and often the pain inflicted is more than physical pain and the damage it causes can be more permanent.

Destroying an elbow joint or bouncing someone's brain off the inside of their skull is comparatively easy, but it's far more difficult to decide whether or not it is appropriate to inflict even more pain and damage by telling the absolute truth.

Truth… you can only be true to yourself, but remember, no one believes a liar even when they are telling the truth and when truth is replaced by silence, that silence is often a lie.

"More crea you can s

Based in the heart of Manchester Rowlinson Broughton was one of the oldest and largest advertising agencies in Europe. 1968 - here I am, straight out of art college and thrown in at the deep end.

...ive talent than ...ake a stick at!"

I am , of course, referring to the 4 other gentlemen in this photograph and not yours truly, the beardless 20 year old whelp in the foreground.

Here I am at the commencement of a perilous ascent up the greasy, slippery, slimy slope of the archetypal 'Ad Man'. Straight out of Art College to Studio junior to Designer to Art director to Creative director. The permed hair, the Porsche, the Armani suits, the Filofax and of course the 3 hour liquid lunches. I had the lot and I got away with it for years, but it filled me with a questionable sense of pride.

I had a love hate relationship with my years as an advertising man in the big agencies. I loved the creativity, and still do, but I hated the bullshit, and the fact that once upon a time people needed stuff to survive, but because of advertising, stuff now needs people.

My old Dad used to say "for God's sake son, don't tell your Mother you work in Advertising, 'cos she thinks you play the piano in a brothel."

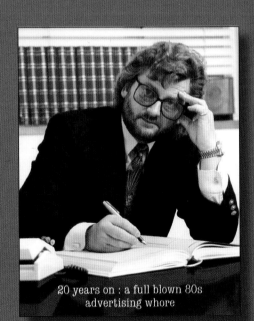

20 years on : a full blown 80s advertising whore

A Manchester

Piccadilly Gardens in Manchester City Centre - circa 1960.
On the top left hand side of the picture you will see Royal Buildings and under the Capstan
sign a half round window - I sat in that window for 5 years working as an artist with
Rowlinson Broughton, as mentioned on the previous page.

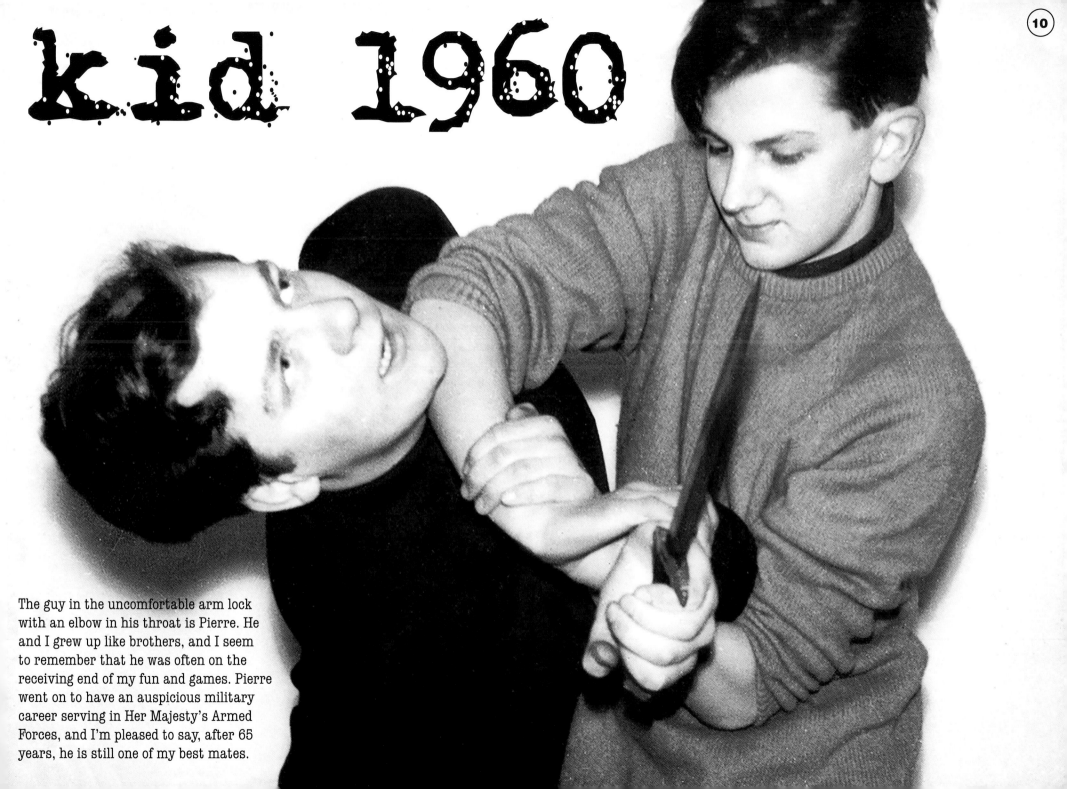

kid 1960

The guy in the uncomfortable arm lock with an elbow in his throat is Pierre. He and I grew up like brothers, and I seem to remember that he was often on the receiving end of my fun and games. Pierre went on to have an auspicious military career serving in Her Majesty's Armed Forces, and I'm pleased to say, after 65 years, he is still one of my best mates.

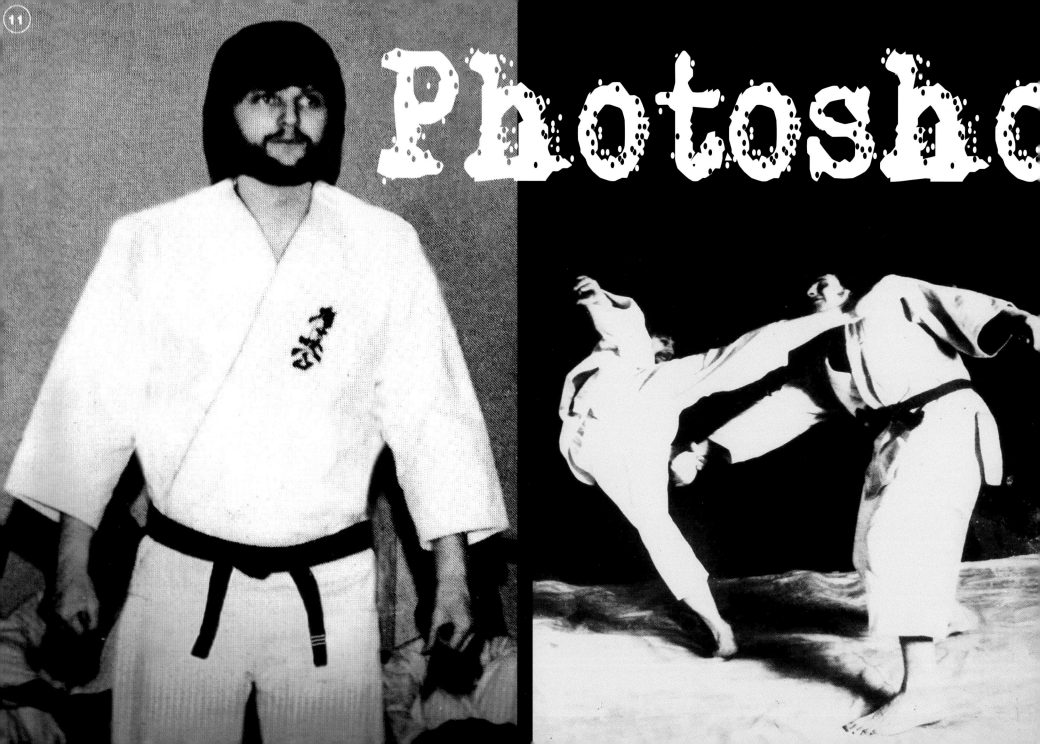

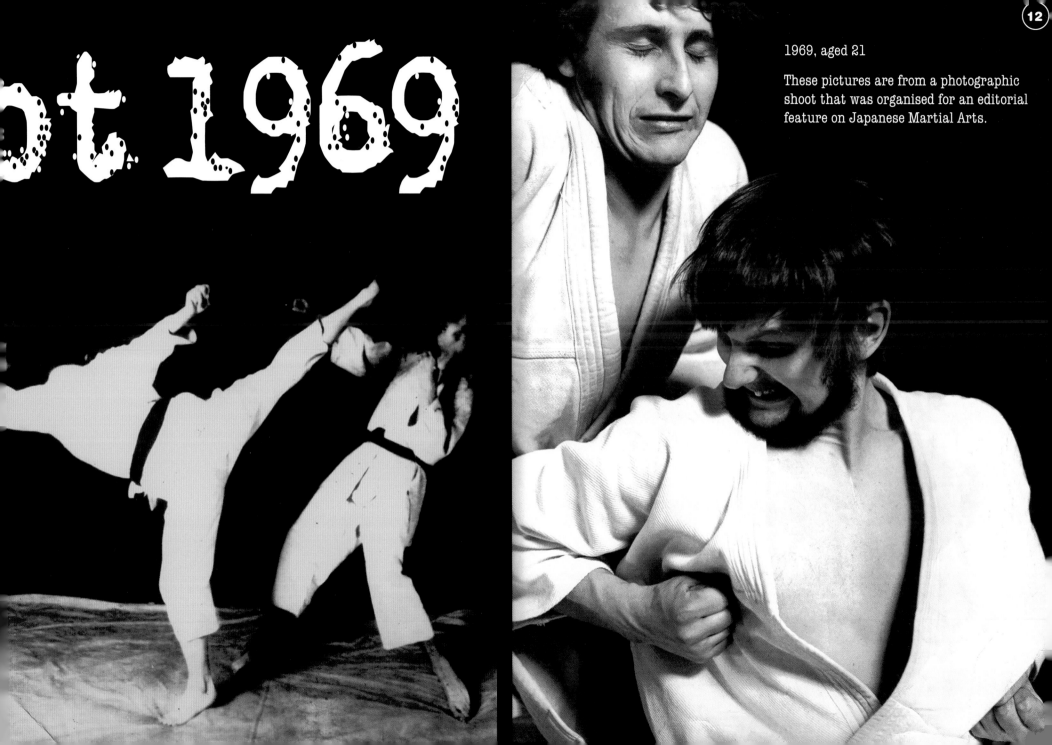

ot 1969

1969, aged 21

These pictures are from a photographic shoot that was organised for an editorial feature on Japanese Martial Arts.

13

Practicing 'Tameshiwari', the practice of testing the power of a striking technique by breaking solid objects (don't know why I did it, because it hurt like hell).

"i may not look tough, but i can definitely spoil your day"

"I believe training to deal with violence is essential, but I also believe that training to recognise what leads up to violence to be at the very core to surviving it.

It is my opinion that the person that is aware of danger in advance of an attack can take control. The person that knows when to fight and when not to fight can take control. The person who recognises and takes advantage of their assailant's weaknesses and is empowered by their own strengths can take control. The person who knows how to handle the superior assailant as well as the inferior assailant can take control, and the person who understands an assailant's spirit as well as they understand their own can take control.

This is the essence of R.E.A.C.T

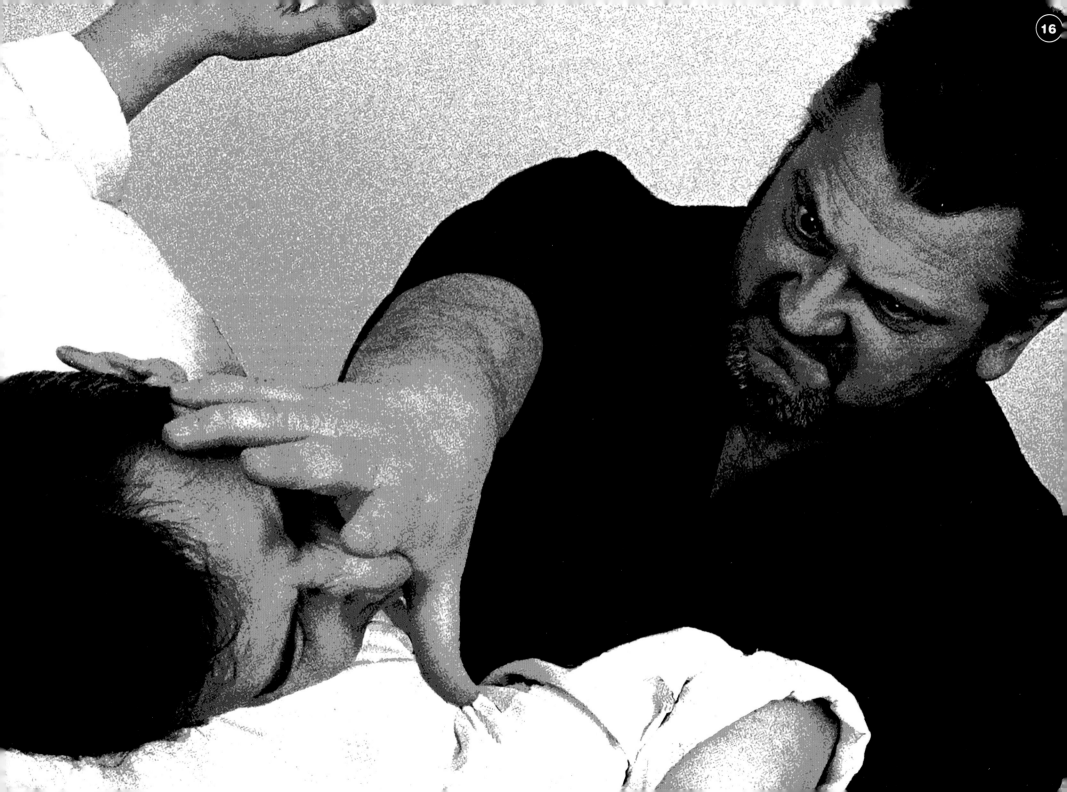

As I've said, I started training in the martial arts when I was 7 years old, I was just a kid; I did it because I was told I was doing it by my best mates Dad and therefore had no preconceived ideas for boosting my self-esteem or developing a big ego, it was just rough and tumble fun. Over the years, however, it has been my experience that martial arts has a tendency to attract a certain type of person, who's goals are often based on insecurity. They would say things such as "I took up martial arts because I was bullied at school"; "I want to learn how to fight"; "I want to be strong and fearless"; "I want to be like James Bond." Unfortunately, this is how all the martial arts ego bullshit gets started, and we all know martial arts Dojos are, more often than not, swarming with people with gigantic egos, but little else, and sometimes the instructors are the worst culprits. Believe me, a punch in the mouth that breaks your teeth will kill an ego stone dead in the blink of an eye, no matter how many black belts you have.

After 30 plus years of training, I started to develop my own ideas for a system of self-defence that had nothing to prove, and therefore no ego. I called it R.E.A.C.T.

R.E.A.C.T is not a martial art, bogged down with an out-dated arsenal of 2000 plus techniques. Nor is R.E.A.C.T a method of fighting, it is simply a way of thinking and acting to avoid violence but, when necessary, that thought process can be transformed into physical combative tactics. That is why I describe R.E.A.C.T as an 'Ethos Beyond Technique'.

I have never had any interest in teaching people how to fight, but I will teach them how, by following the logic of my R.E.A.C.T system, they can take control and terminate hostility, aggressive confrontation and, when necessary, the physical violence of an actual attack.

A.C.T

"An Ethos Beyond Technique"

ETHOS

BEYOND TECHNIQUE

I designed this logo for the R.E.A.C.T Specialist Training my company delivers.

THINK SAFE, ACT SAFE, STAY SAFE
R·E·A·C·T

In 1997, after 40 years of study and training in the martial arts, I was commissioned by the publisher Harper Collins to be the technical adviser and co-writer of the 'SAS Self Defence' book. In 2001 Harper Collins then commissioned me to write my own book on personal protection and self defence, which I titled 'Think Safe, Act Safe, Stay Safe with REACT', which went on to become one of the best selling books of its type ever published. The following text is the introduction to the first R.E.A.C.T book.

In the absence of a utopian society where everybody loves his neighbour, the sun always shines and bluebirds fill the skies, every man, woman and child on the planet needs some way of defending themselves. In fact, we all perform defensive strategies in our daily lives without even being aware of it. The child who walks a different way to school each morning to avoid the class bully is actually implementing a defensive strategy. Putting your seat belt on when you get into your car is a defensive strategy. Flinching and yelling out when startled is also a form of defensive strategy. It is part of our natural instinct to survive.

Most of us have a natural built-in instinct to try and avoid trouble if we possibly can. However, the sad but stark reality is that violent crime has become a worldwide social disease of epidemic proportions. It has been steadily on the increase over the last fifty years. Children are murdered or subjected to horrific cruelty and abuse, old ladies are raped in their sick beds, young women are regularly savaged in public places, men and boys are beaten, stabbed and shot to death on our streets every day. I am not qualified to even attempt to try and explain why this is, or moralise about the state of today's society, but what I can say, without fear of contradiction, is that it will probably get worse before it even starts to get better. Thus, if you accept this you owe it to yourself to learn how to increase your chances of survival. We've all read about the needless suffering of innocent people time and time again and yet, in the majority of cases, with a little knowledge these people could have avoided a violent and dangerous situation. Living in a jungle doesn't mean you should accept the role of prey to the predators that are, without doubt, out there.

How many times have you thought 'it will never happen to me' or 'well, if it's going to happen it's going to happen, there's nothing I can do about it'? Has your religion conditioned you to 'turn the other cheek'? All of these attitudes will get you into deep trouble on the streets. It might just happen to you; in fact, statistics show there is a strong possibility that it will. But if it's going to

happen there is something you can do about it. Co-operate with a mugger and you will be mugged, co-operate with a rapist and you will be raped, co-operate with a murderer and you will be murdered, and that 'turn the other cheek' thing means you just get that one punched as well, or worse still, slashed with a knife.

Most large cities have seen a rapid decline in people's respect for one another, resulting in aggression, selfishness and a huge number of individuals living in constant fear of attack. Despite this increase in violence most people mistakenly believe that it is the job of the police to protect us from harm. That's where we're wrong – it is the job of the police to enforce and uphold the laws of the country. It is up to us to take steps to ensure our own safety and that of our family. There are people out there who were never endowed with a social conscience; the only pain they acknowledge is their own. The sociopaths are all around us, the problem is that they look just like you and I. They are society's predators and they will always prey on the weak, or what they perceive to be a 'soft' target. The behaviour of these types can range from the manipulator, whose sole purpose is self-gratification at the expense, or even pain of others, to the extreme of the serial killer. Their primary characteristics are that they have no regard for anybody, other than what they can take from them. The sociopath will happily beat their victim to a pulp without feeling one second of remorse or guilt. These predators want your property, your body, your life or all three, and believe it is their right to take any, or all of them.

But let's be positive. You do not have to accept that it's inevitable you will fall prey to these people. Don't adopt a passive stance, although you must accept that you will probably, at some time in your life, come into contact with a situation that may be potentially dangerous. This isn't to say that you should take the law into your own hands, but it does mean that you should take responsibility for your own protection and arm yourself with the knowledge and ability to do so. Very few things happen on the streets that aren't detectable in advance, but if you're not alert and aware you won't see the danger signs.

So what can you do?

Most people automatically think of the martial arts such as judo, jujutsu, karate and aikido, which is fine as far as it goes. I have been involved in the martial arts, in one way or another, since 1956. I am the proud owner of literally hundreds of books on the subject. I have studied, practised and taught the martial arts for most of my life. I have had the privilege of training with some of the world's most eminent masters and authorities and I would like to think I have achieved a reasonably high level of competence. One thing is for sure, I have loved every minute of it and wouldn't have missed this experience for the world. However, in truth, out of the thousands of techniques and combinations taught – strikes, kicks, punches, projections, pins, chokes, throws, locks and neutralisations, few are relevant in a real-life street situation.

Being a martial artist does not mean you are able to defend yourself. The techniques a traditional practitioner studies and may even become highly skilled in, can be your worst enemy in a real fight. Two or three instinctive and well-practised moves are all you actually need. Please don't think I am saying martial arts are a waste of time; they are not and a good grounding in them gives you a degree of physical fitness, good reflexes, good balance, good timing and an awareness others don't possess. The main problem is that most of the martial arts are taught and practised as sports, with a small amount of self-defence thrown in for good measure and to make it a bit more interesting. Unfortunately, the self-defence is not usually very realistic and is based on classical and formalised attacks and defence techniques, and so much of the self-defence taught in martial arts schools only works if your training partner allows it to.

Remember that martial arts, self-defence and fighting are three very different things. A martial art is just that – an art.

Practitioners spend a lifetime practising and perfecting highly complex combat techniques. Even many of today's supremely skilled masters are only masters of modern, watered-down adaptations of the original combat systems developed for the battlefield. These original combat skills were for fighting, while the modern martial arts we know today are designed for study and not for combat. In self-defence the goal is to avoid harm, to survive. In self-defence it should be completely unnecessary to confront and in fact, it is preferable that we don't confront unless it is absolutely unavoidable. Even if physical confrontation becomes inevitable you must extract yourself at the first possible opportunity. For 'extract yourself' read 'run away'. The best place to be when 'the shit hits the fan' is somewhere else! This may not be good for your ego, but we are talking self-defence, self-preservation. Don't endanger yourself and others by fighting just to prove that you can, and don't confuse ego with honour. Honour is your strength of character and your integrity. No-one can take that from you. Your ego, on the other hand, can get you hurt or even killed. You must look on self-defence as a necessity and understand how to minimise the risk of an attack.

The aim of fighting is to defeat an opponent or an enemy. Soldiers fight: it's their job to kill or even be killed if necessary, for their country. A boxer fights, some are paid huge amounts of money to get knocked around the ring and hopefully come out on top. So, unless you are a professional fighter there should never be any need to do it, but if you are faced with having to fight remember that a real fight on the street rarely lasts more than 20 seconds, it is not a game and there are no rules. You must take control.

So how do we do that? How do we give ourselves the edge that enables us to walk away from a nasty situation, preferably unharmed? You need to be aware that human behaviour, both your own and your assailant's, can't be predicted with any degree of certainty, particularly in a stressful situation, so there's no point in pretending it's easy, or there's some mystical, magic wand that

will make it all go away. Don't kid yourself that you will leap into action with fists of fury and vanquish your assailant. You won't. But there are things you can do and they are summed up in one little word – REACT.

REACT is not just a clever name thought up by marketing people; it is a system that enables you to stay in tune with your environment, to be relaxed but alert, aware of your surroundings and switched on to any escalation in your personal threat level. REACT is a defensive strategy, not a martial art or a method of fighting. In fact you could say it's a system of how to avoid fighting and that's exactly my aim in writing this book, to teach you how to avoid conflict and confrontation. If, however, all your preventive efforts fail and you do face an actual attack, I will also show you some simple yet effective techniques and tactics to help you act to your best advantage in the event of a violent attack.

Most of you reading this book will drive a car and many of you will have driven for years and travelled tens of thousands of miles. Every time you get into your vehicle, fasten your seat belt and commence your journey, whether you are aware of it or not, you apply the principles of REACT. You are conditioned to recognise that driving from A to B could be potentially dangerous. So what do you do? You switch on, you become more aware, you look ahead, you look behind, you become acutely aware of other vehicles, intersections, side streets, road signs, traffic lights, pedestrian crossings, children. In fact a huge amount of visual and mental stimulus is being processed by you, and all at thirty, forty, fifty miles per hour or more. And why? Because it's instinctive. You do it automatically in order to maintain your progress and arrive at your destination safe and in one piece by avoiding an accident. Why not apply this attitude of mind when you are walking around? At three miles per hour it should be much easier! The REACT system helps you to remember, the REACT system helps you to switch on to your environment.

THINK ACT STAY SAFE

BE YOUR OWN GUARDIAN ANGEL WITH THE

R·E·A·C·T

APPROACH TO SELF-DEFENCE

STEVE COLLINS

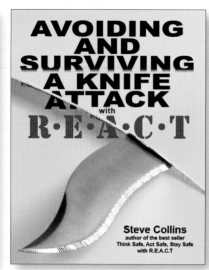

AVOIDING AND SURVIVING A KNIFE ATTACK

with

R·E·A·C·T

Steve Collins
author of the best seller
Think Safe, Act Safe, Stay Safe
with R.E.A.C.T

STEVE COLLINS

Author of the best selling
'Self defence & Personal
Safety with R.E.A.C.T'
is now keeping you
one step ahead
of the game
with his

R.E.A.C.T
SURVIVAL FILES

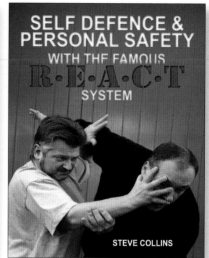

SELF DEFENCE & PERSONAL SAFETY

WITH THE FAMOUS

R·E·A·C·T

SYSTEM

STEVE COLLINS

R·E·A·C·T TEACHER'S

Steve Collins

Weapons and violence in schools

Living in an Age of Terrorism

Student's Handbook

Protocols and Procedures
to deal with a
Terrorist Attack and its Aftermath

Presented by
PS5

R·E·A·C·T
AN ETHOS BEYOND TECHNIQUE

The R·E·A·C·T System of
Confrontation Management & Personal Protection

By
Steve Collins

First Edition 2017

R·E·A·C·T
AN ETHOS BEYOND TECHNIQUE

The system of
Confrontation Management & Personal Protection

By
Steve Collins

Second Edition 2016

**Basic Firearms
Recognition &
Safety Procedures**

**Creating
Safer Communities
through
Weapons Awareness**

by Steve Collins

RULES FOR DEALING WITH AN ACTIVE SHOOTER

R·E·A·C·T
PERSONAL SAFETY
SECURITY LIBRARY

**Simple
Guidelines**

Steve Collins

Weapons Awareness & Recognition

**Master
Trainer's Manual**

By
Steve Collins

**R·E·A·C·T
Training Manual**

By
Steve Collins

THE

R·E·A·C·T-OR

COMPLIANCE TOOL

TRAINING
MANUAL

Part of the PS5 Organisation

©PS5/Steve Collins

THE ESSENCE OF
SECURITY SEARCH

Source Reference

By Steve Collins

R·E·A·C·T

VERBAL

Handling verbal aggression

Steve Collins

R·E·A·C·T

JUNIOR

Keeping your children safe

Steve Collins

R·E·A·C·T

Travel

The key to safer travel

Steve Collins

Issue 31 — This Special Issue is part of the PS5 Weapons Awareness & Recognition Programmes 2015

PCW REVIEW
PROTECTING CITIZENS WORLDWIDE
The PS5 Journal

THE DANGERS OF CONCEALED WEAPONS

CONFERENCE EDITION

THE PS5 TRAINING

Protecting Citizens Worldwide

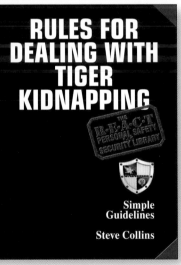

RULES FOR DEALING WITH TIGER KIDNAPPING

THE R·E·A·C·T PERSONAL SAFETY SECURITY LIBRARY

Simple Guidelines

Steve Collins

RULES FOR DEALING WITH AN ARMED ROBBERY

THE R·E·A·C·T PERSONAL SAFETY SECURITY LIBRARY

Steve Collins

RULES FOR DEALING WITH VERBAL & PHYSICAL CONFRONTATION

THE R·E·A·C·T PERSONAL SAFETY SECURITY LIBRARY

Steve Collins

RULES FOR DEALING WITH AN ARMED ROBBERY

THE R·E·A·C·T PERSONAL SAFETY SECURITY LIBRARY *Vehicle Edition*

Steve Collins

RULES FOR DEALING WITH RETAIL CRIME

THE R·E·A·C·T PERSONAL SAFETY SECURITY LIBRARY

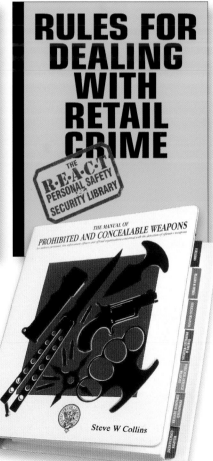

THE MANUAL OF PROHIBITED AND CONCEALABLE WEAPONS

Steve W Collins

My Books, Publications & Training Manuals

Stand tall in the face of adversity

This powerful image epitomises the philosophy that lies at the heart of my REACT personal safety training and educational programmes. The ethos behind 'Standing Tall in the Face of Adversity' is simple and teaches us to understand that, no matter how black and hopeless things appear, we always have options; and the realisation that you may not be looking defeat in the face is empowering. I have continuously marketed the concept of REACT and of Standing Tall in the Face of Adversity for over 2 decades and on the following double page spread you will see just some of the advertising and marketing concepts we have designed and produced in the in-house PS5 creative studios

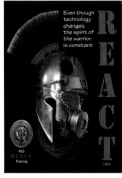

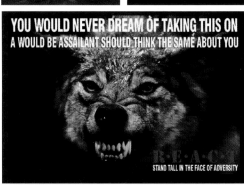

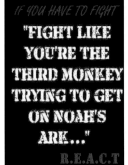

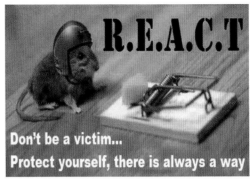

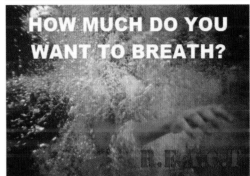

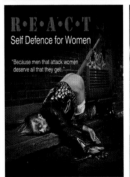

"True Victory is Self Victory"

Caligraphy by Morihei Ueshiba - O Sensei
1883 - 1969

The Void

Japanese calligraphy
depicting 'the void'

The Book of Five Rings, was written by Japanese master swordsman Miyamoto Musashi in 1645, and is one of the world's classic sources of strategy. Even today its influence extends far beyond mere martial strategy into the entire Japanese business culture.

The Book of the Void is the final chapter of Musashi's book, following the Ground Book, the Water Book, the Fire Book, and the Wind Book.

Musashi said – 'What I call the void is where nothing exists. It is about things outside man's knowledge. Of course the void does not exist. By knowing what exists, you can know that which does not exist. This is the void..'

If you are wondering what that means, my interpretation of the Book of the Void is that it's about strategy based on the natural instinct of a clear and empty mind rather than the reasoned thought of the cognitive mind.

You can gain tactical knowledge by study and relentless training and practice; and of course this is a necessity to maintain your edge. However, if you only focus on the physical realm you will neither decipher the meaning of 'the void', nor the meaning at the heart of my R.E.A.C.T system and therefore struggle to broaden your knowledge and skills.

"

There is an old expression that goes: "Be the water not the rock" and I believe this quote sums up my R.E.A.C.T System perfectly.
Picture, if you can, a river meandering its way through the landscape. Now picture a large rock standing right in the middle of the water, trying to stem its flow.
Unfortunately this describes how many people try to deal with conflict. They stand in the middle of the torrent like a big rock and try to stop the onslaught, but, just like water, it keeps on coming. The water is unyielding and uncompromising, it has power, flexibility and direction, but the rock is stubborn, immovable and inflexible; as a result the rock is eventually, little by little, worn down and down and down by the water until it becomes a pebble.
We have all started the day feeling like a rock and ready for anything the world can throw at us, but many of us have gone to our beds feeling like a pebble having been worn down by the unrelenting onslaught of the trials and tribulations of the day.

So try and be the water, not the rock and let it flow from you like a river, not forcing, but not holding back.

5 Steps to Becoming a Victim

1 Intent

The decision has been made to commit violence in order to obtain a goal. Often a person who has decided to launch a physical assault will either look for a reason or excuse to attack, or will try and hide their intentions until they are ready. Fortunately, despite the exterior appearances, many times there is enough non-verbal communication coming from an attacker to warn you that something is wrong. People have to undergo certain physiological changes for the body to be ready to attack or defend. These are reflected in a person's body language. While they can be very subtle, they are recognizable to an observer, either consciously or unconsciously. Trust your gut instinct. Often your subconscious recognises the physiological danger signals being displayed. Even if a situation looks normal but your alarm bells go off, do not ignore it, and start to look for the next two stages developing before its too late. Knowing and understanding this process serves as an early warning system for the recognition of the danger signs. Your attacker's body will tell you he's about to attack, even if the words are calm and normal.

2 The Interview

Remember the assailant's personal safety is a critical factor in deciding whether or not he attacks you. The 'interview' is where the decision of whether or not he is safe to attack is being considered. If for one moment the criminal thought an attack would be unsuccessful they will almost certainly move on and seek easier prey. "Will I succeed?" That is a major incentive for what any one of us decides to do or not do. The 'interview' is the test, and this is one interview you definitely want to fail. By failing, the assailant will decide that he cannot successfully, or easily, attack you. There are four basic types of interviews.

Innocent

This is the most common. The approach is often under the guise of an innocent request, i.e. needing information, a light or the time. This is a distraction. While they are talking, they are not only getting in position to attack, but checking your awareness of what they are doing and your commitment to defending yourself.

Threatening

You are minding your own business one minute, and the next you have a threatening, obscenity screaming person in your face. The success of this strategy relies on you not being accustomed to dealing with extreme emotional and verbal abuse and reacting in a stunned and confused manner.

Escalating

Unlike the threatening interview, which starts out immediately hostile, an escalating interview starts out normally, but it rapidly turns hostile. The person is testing your boundaries by escalating offensive behaviour. The more they get away with, the more the behaviour escalates and becomes more and more extreme until finally they attack. This is a very common interview technique for date rapists. It is also common with groups of loitering youths looking for trouble.

Hushed

the street predators put themselves in a position to observe you. They may never speak until the attack, but they have been watching and observing you for some time. They may position themselves out of sight in order to follow you. Or they may make their presence known and decide to attack if you show any signs of fear.

3 Positioning

This is the predator putting himself/herself in a place where they can successfully attack you. Typical street robbers are cowards and do not want to fight you; they want to overwhelm you with intimidation and fear. To accomplish this, they have to put themselves into a position where they can do it quickly and effectively. Positioning is the final proof that someone is trying to put themselves into a place from which to attack, and therefore removes all doubt that the situation is innocent. You will seldom, if ever, be mugged in the middle of a crowd. Therefore a key point of all positioning is what I call the 'fringe areas'. A fringe area is where you could be close to people, but out of range of immediate help. You may not get robbed in the middle of a busy shopping centre, but could be in the car park, toilets, or the stairwells. All these should be considered potential positioning danger areas. Even a separate room in a crowded house can constitute a fringe area, as many women who have been raped at a party will testify. There are three basic types of positioning for a single assailant:

Reducing the gap

The most basic form of positioning is simply walking up to the victim. The closer you allow a criminal to get, the greater their ability to overwhelm and control you.

Trapping

This is the most common. He/she approaches you from a direction that traps you between himself and a large object, like a car or wall etc. This also entails putting themselves between you and an escape route.

Surprise

The classic ambush. The assailants position themselves in places where you can't see them, or certainly not until the last moment. From this position, they can easily step out and attack. Once you know these types of locations, this kind of positioning is relatively easy to thwart.

4 The Attack

If the first three stages have been achieved, there is no reason for the street predators not to use violence to get what they want from you. Many robberies and rapes are committed with the simple threat of, or just a display of, violence. A violent, verbal outburst will not physically harm the victim, but clearly indicates that unless he or she cooperates, the victim will be hurt. Weapons can be displayed to convince a victim to cooperate. Other attacks are no more than brutal and outright physical assaults. Such attacks can come both with and without warning. At its most extreme, it means the criminal simply walking up to someone with a gun and pulling the trigger. Unfortunately, there is no way to determine which one you will encounter. An attack can turn from one type to another in a heartbeat. What was just a verbal threat a second ago, can explode into deadly violence.

5 The Impulse

This is how the predator feels about what they have done. In the aftermath of mugging someone, the street robber could decide on pure impulse or just a whim, to beat, stab or shoot you despite the fact that you have cooperated fully and offered no resistance.

Of these impulsive reactions, one of the most consistently dangerous is one that occurs amongst rapists. If the rapist feels that the rape was not as satisfying as they hoped it would be, extreme violence often occurs. It is a fact a large percentage of women who have been raped are seriously harmed by the rapists after the actual sexual assault.

This puts paid to the 'lay back and think of England' theory. In any circumstance, until the assailant is completely out of your sight, you are still at risk of the impulsive reaction to hurt you still more, even though you have been totally cooperative. The unpredictability of the criminal's reaction is another reason why it is far easier to avoid violence than it is to try to extract yourself safely from the middle of it.

Conclusion

Knowing these five stages is a consistent guide by which you can assess the potential threat of a situation. The stages are inherent within crime and violence. The stages give you an external set of standards to check against someone's behaviour. If the collective behaviour is present, you are, indeed, in danger and need to take steps to ensure your safety. You need to do this no matter what is being said, since actions almost always speak louder than words.

There is no one thing that will inform you that you are in danger. This is why the five stage checklist is so reliable. A single element might be misconstrued or explained away. However, you will never get the collective presence of all five accidentally.

"Apathy and Denial will kill you

The first time is that 'holy shit' moment of truth.. that sudden realisation that you have done nothing to physically or psychologically prepare yourself for this moment.

Your only strategy was...

"..it won't happen to me"

..and now it's happening!

The second time is because, even if you survive, for the rest of your life you will carry the physical and/or emotional scars that will constantly remind you that you could have done something to protect yourself if only you had been bothered to find out how.

twice!"

"There is no such thing as women's self defence"

Marble relief showing female gladiators, named Amazonia and Achillia. Each carries a short sword and a shield. (Roman, 1st–2nd century AD) British Museum.
Female gladiators were the creation of men as a reflection of male fascination and curiosity. However, their battles in the arena were often as equally brutal to the men's. Women were also members of the 'Venatores', (gladiators who fought wild animals in the arena).

I have been teaching personal protection and self defence for a very long time, and it is my considered opinion that there are hundreds of common misconceptions regarding the subject of women's self defence.

One of the most common, and it tends to put most women off completely right from the start, is that they will have to stand in a cold Church hall with a load of sweaty guys and learn some type of 'martial art'. This is of course completely erroneous.

In fact taking up a classical martial art as a means of learning self defence is a complete waste of time and probably the worst thing anyone could do, male or female. I have studied, practised and taught the martial arts for over 50 years. I have had the privilege of training with some of the world's most eminent masters and authorities.

However, the truth is that out of the thousands of martial arts techniques that exist very few are relevant in a real-life 21st century violent situation.

Bizarrely, being a martial artist does not indicate you are necessarily capable of defending yourself. It is a fact that the majority of martial arts practitioners, black belts included, have little to no street self defence experience or skills.

The techniques a traditional martial arts practitioner studies, and in some cases become highly skilled in, can in fact become their worst enemy in a real situation outside the dojo or training hall.

The main problem is that martial arts are generally taught and practised as sports, with a bit of self defence thrown in for good measure (if you're lucky). Unfortunately, the self defence is not usually very realistic and often based on classical and formalised attacks and defence techniques. And to make matters worse it is habitually taught from the point of attack, which of course is too late.

Martial arts, self defence and fighting are three very different things.

A martial art is just that, an art. Practitioners can spend a lifetime training to perfect highly complex techniques.

Even many of today's supremely skilled masters are only masters of modern, watered down adaptations of the original combat systems that were invented and developed for the battlefield. If a Self defence technique is so complex that you need to practice it for years, then it is too complicated for use in a real attack situation, however, if a Self defence strategy is simple enough to be effective with minimal training, then it's simple enough to use effectively on the street....

Another false belief held by many ladies is that women cannot defend themselves against a man.

I hear all too often..."If a big guy grabbed me, I'd never be able to get him off." Sadly this is another widely held misconception and the vast majority of women have some sort of in-built feeling of defencelessness when it comes to the thought of having to protect themselves from a big powerful man. They often think they need to possess an ability to unleash punches and kicks with immense physical power, or be able to execute sophisticated martial art techniques....
...None of this is true!

"Self Defence Training specially designed for the ladies"

There are those that promote themselves as experts in 'Self Defence for Women'.

In my opinion this is a real danger area, as I do not believe there is any such thing as 'women's self defence'.

There are no special rules that only apply to women. There are no clandestine strategies or secret techniques that are especially effective when used by a woman. Female Military combative's are not trained to fight differently than their male comrades. Female Police PSUs are not trained in different riot control techniques than the men they stand shoulder to shoulder with in the line and the C&R taught to women Prison officers is exactly the same as that taught to the guys.

Even the term women's self defence gives the impression that women have to have some special type of training in order for them to be capable of protecting themselves. Not true!

Therefore, what I mean when I say that women's self defence does not exist is that I do not believe there is any difference between the way a woman should defend herself and the way a man defends himself.

We have all heard or even used the term "She's one of the lads". Well, when it comes to women defending themselves that phrase just about sums it up. Street predators, robbers and rapists tend to enjoy success because they are more or less willing to do anything and everything to achieve their goals.

If their victims are hurt, injured, maimed or mortally wounded, they either don't care or are actually quite proud of the results, and that ethos not only applies to their male victims but also or should I say 'especially' applies to their female victims. If someone decides they are going to harm you whether it's for pleasure or profit, don't think for one second that they're going to pull any punches because you're a young girl or an old lady. NO! You are the prey and they are the predator, and for that moment in time a women under attack becomes just one of the lads. She may as well be a man because that's the way she will be treated.

Methods of attack do not discriminate by gender so why should the way a woman defends herself differ.

An attacker can only want one, or a combination of three things, 'your property', 'your body' or 'your life'. The fact there may be a sexual element to an attack on a woman should only strengthen her resolve to act in the same manner as her attacker and defend with extreme prejudice.

I say again. Women's self defence does NOT exist.

Become the Predator

The 'Become the Predator' rule applies to everyone, but it especially applies to females. Adopting a mindset that you will not under any circumstances whatsoever become a victim and knowing beforehand that if faced with a violent situation, you will become the predator is the key and not some silly martial art technique.

Being a predator may seem a little alien. But you must have the conviction to apply whatever methods you deem necessary to control the situation without a flicker of hesitation. Think of yourself as being higher up the food chain than this chunk of detritus attempting to invade your life. Turn them into your prey.

In an imminently violent situation your choices are limited, run away if you can, submit or fight. If you do run, run like a cheetah, but if you have to fight, fight like a tiger protecting her cubs.

What do all predators have in common?

'They attack, they do not defend'.

They are the aggressors and finding themselves suddenly having to defend just happens to be an assailant's worst nightmare. If they thought for one second that their female victims were going to successfully fight back, they would not have considered attacking them in the first place. You must give yourself permission to take control. Reject the role of prey and become the predator.

Remember, the reason street predators are successful is that they are willing to do almost anything to overwhelm their victims with unbridled raw violence. Whilst the law abiding citizen, tends to be concerned about whether they might injure their attacker by fighting back.

If a woman wants to survive a violent attack, all she needs do is visualise the kind of brutality and damage an attacker would, without hesitation, try to inflict on her. The defence mechanisms have to be pitched, at a level even higher.

Situation Awareness

All successful self defence begins a long time before any physical attack takes place. The most powerful preventative tactics any of us have against being attacked are:

An awareness of your surroundings and location is the cornerstone of good personal security. It is much easier to stay out of trouble than it is to get out of trouble. If you are ignorant of your environment you may as well walk around wearing a great big neon sign saying 'VICTIM'.

Situation awareness is the ability to recognise potentially dangerous environments, but be aware that some of the most peaceful-looking locations can still be affected by crime.

Nowhere should be thought of as being completely safe. A developed sense of situation awareness will not only help you keep out of trouble, but also give you some options to escape from it.

Threat Awareness

Understanding the dangers that may be lurking in the shadows of your surroundings is paramount, but don't let your location threaten you more than an actual attack. A knife at your throat in a multi-storey car park, a knife at your throat on the riverbank or a knife at your throat in your own home is still a fucking knife at your throat. The place makes no difference to the severity of the attack. So, as situation awareness is being aware of your location, threat awareness is being aware of the people in your location. It's the

predator that will hurt you, not the dark alleyway.

Threat awareness is your early warning system. It is essential that you know what is going on all around you all the time. The quicker you become aware of a problem the less likely it is to take you by surprise. Street robbers and rapists are predators. Many non-violent criminals, burglars and thieves are opportunists. Predators will look for the weakest animal in the herd. When you stay aware of what is happening and who is around you, the street predators lose their element of surprise.

Confidence to fight back

When it comes to an actual attack the best defence is just not to be there in the first place. However, if your back is against the wall, you have to have a tactical edge and that will not materialise through hours and hours of inappropriate martial arts training.

Learning half a dozen simple but highly effective dirty tricks is all you need. Just knowing that you have these tricks at your fingertips and ready for use at all times, augmented by the fact that you know they work, is incredibly empowering and instils the confidence to fight back. I feel it's very condescending to women that there are those out there that believe a woman should not fight back.

They say "Oh, you shouldn't fight back because you'll be too weak and scared to be affective, just escape". Now I'm a firm believer in the running away philosophy, but in reality if some guy is pinning you down, punching you in the face, threatening to kill you and ripping your clothes off ...where are you going to run to?

A Woman's Ultimate Weapon is her brain. The knowledge she needs to protect herself should be in her head not her biceps. Time and effort is required to gain this knowledge. Trying to hone the body into a female gladiator is totally unnecessary, but what is crucial is the empowerment that gives you permission to take control.

Ok, so as a rule women are not as strong as men, but the fact is that on the whole women tend to be smarter than men, possess more guile than men, have a higher pain threshold than men, and be more flexible than men, plus women possess a capacity to be much more ruthless than most men can ever be. Add to this some basic physiological facts regarding the vulnerability of a man's body.

So please beware of those that market their system as one with specially developed self defence techniques just for women, because it's Bull Shit...."Women's Self Defence Does Not Exist"

"My 5 R.E.A.C.T
Rules for Women"

1. **Your friend is not always a friend**

More than 70% of rapes and sexual assaults on women are perpetrated by someone they know, and more than 50% of attacks take place either in or close to the victim's own home.

2. **There are always warning signs**

The vast majority of attacks are preceded by some form of verbal assault. I call this the 'Interview'. Knowing how to recognise and deal with the warning signs that the Interview sends out can help you avert many attacks from ever becoming physical.

3. **Try to have a silver tongue**

Talking can often do the trick. Reason, diplomacy, tact and a little psychology even compassion and sympathy can go a long way to subduing a potentially violent situation. The verbal defuse is a powerful tool and a few carefully chosen words can sometimes make all the difference. I call it 'Verbal Interaction Control' or VIC for short.

4. **Hit & Run**

Get away as quickly as you possibly can. The Hit & Run principle has nothing to do with fighting. It means you must do something that interrupts the attackers thought pattern. Hit him with an assertive and confident yell…NO!!!! Or ask a question that makes him stop and think for a moment, it only takes a split second to breakaway and run. If you have no choice but to physically hit your attacker, go for his eyes. 90% of the time a short sharp jab in the eye with a finger nail is all you will need to create enough time to escape.

5. **Fight like a Tiger protecting her Cubs**

A nasty situation is rapidly growing uglier. You have tried to talk your way out, but to no avail, and you seem to have no means of escape. What can you do now?

Remember, Men that attack Women have no scruples and will not attack a Woman any differently than they would attack a Man.

If you fear for your safety or even your life, and there is no other option, you must FIGHT and do it with extreme prejudice, using any means at your disposal. Your goal is always to get away, but to achieve this the assailant needs to feel like they've just been hit by a truck they didn't see coming.

Strive to become a techni not a fi

The R.E.A.C.T Dynamic Spiral

The physics behind the System

The Pauli

$$\Psi_1(x, t) - \Psi_2(x, t)$$

Exclusion Principle

The Pauli Exclusion Principle states that by the laws of physics two objects cannot occupy the same space at the same time.

I utilised this principle for my REACT System and called it 'The REACT Windows of Opportunity'.

Imagine your body is split into 4 sections or windows. Think of a vertical line from the top of your head to your toes and a horizontal line at your navel - splitting your body into 4 separate sections.

As the Exclusion Principle proves, it is impossible for two objects to occupy the same space at the same time and as it is unlikely that a would be assailant would attempt to attack through more than 1 window, then by putting your hands into one of the 4 windows, an incoming attack will be stopped or diverted.

This principle has nothing to do with classical martial arts or combat systems, it is pure physics and as I have already stated, you should strive to become a technician not a fighter.

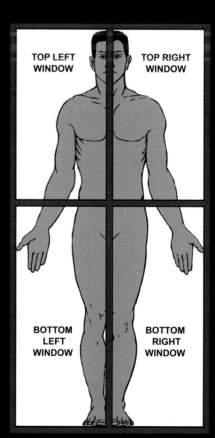

TOP LEFT WINDOW TOP RIGHT WINDOW

BOTTOM LEFT WINDOW BOTTOM RIGHT WINDOW

Although the letter 'T' is the last letter in my R.E.A.C.T acronym, it actually stands for the 'Five Ts of Termination'. Understand that, in order to terminate a situation successfully, whether it be verbally or physically, the principle of the 'Five T's' is crucial.

The 5Ts are :-

- Tools
- Targets
- Tactics
- Techniques
- Terminate

This represents a simple formula for the last resort of all self defence, which is 'physical intervention'. If a confrontation has reached the point that the only way you can protect yourself is to resort to taking physical action, you must have an ethos that is simple to remember, easy to execute and highly effective. The R.E.A.C.T 5 Ts is central to understanding realistic and successful self defence and how to best utilize your body as a weapon.

The 5 T's

"Speak

Jo-jutsu is the art of using a short staff (Jo). Jo-jutsu was reputedly invented by Muso Gonnosuke in the 17th century. Legend tells that using the Jo he was the only person ever to have defeated the legendary swordsman, Miyamoto Musashi, victor of over 60 duels; this is the only record of Musashi ever being defeated. Gonnosuke knocked Musashi unconscious, but spared his life.

Nowadays, I prefer to use a walking cane.

softly and carry a big stick "

This phrase is attributed to the 26th President of the USA, Theodore Roosevelt, in a letter he wrote to Henry L Sprague on January 26 1900. It is a proverbial saying advising the tactic of caution and non-aggression, backed up by the ability to carry out violent action when absolutely necessary.

"If you have no other option, fight like a third monkey trying to get on Noah's Ark."

"Keeping one move ahead of the game"

R·E·A·C·T SURVIVAL FILES

The 'Survival Files' consist of short but succinct feature articles which first appeared as a postscript in my original R.E.A.C.T book. Each one specifically focuses on a particular aspect of personal security and safety. The 'Survival Files,' enable the reader to recognise and evaluate given situations in order to take effective and appropriate action. The files often give clear and logical sets of Do's and Don'ts when faced with certain criteria. The 'Survival Files' have become extremely popular and have appeared in many publications, including official Police magazines under the title 'Street Survival'

Everyone on the planet, man, woman or child, has to face a multitude of dangers throughout their lives. These dangers can seem even more intimidating when you add the pressures of day-to-day urban life. Therefore, it is crucial that we all accept and understand the inherent dangers of our daily lives, whether at home, at work or at play. You must give yourself permission to take control in order to protect yourself, your loved ones and those in your care. The basic strategy at all times is to avoid unnecessary risk or danger whenever possible and learn to be a survivor.

We cannot change the world, however, we can minimise the dangers and risks by taking control of ourselves and our health and also (by using situational awareness) take control of our immediate surroundings. At a very basic level there is a substantial amount we can all do to make our lives a lot safer.

THE URBAN SURVIVAL ASSOCIATION

The REACT Survival Files was also the inspiration for the Urban Survival Association (USA).

The inherent dangers lurking in our urban environment can be just as hostile and intimidating as the deepest darkest jungle or as unforgiving as the driest most barren of deserts.

The Urban Survival Association is a FREE membership club, founded with the sole intention of providing an open forum for information, advice and discussion, in relation to all matters concerning personal safety and the measures and means we can take to minimise the impact of potentially dangerous and destructive situations and events that can and will intrude into daily life.

We are all different; we all have different strengths and weaknesses, physical ability, mental strength, experience, etc. We live in different countries and neighbourhoods, travel through vastly different areas and work in diverse occupations. As a result, our requirements in relation to providing a secure environment for ourselves, our loved ones and those in our care, will be very individual and unique to each person. However, there are basic principles of situational awareness and threat recognition that apply to all. The only certainty is that the threats we all face are increasing day by day. To think differently is naïve, and sadly, the 'it won't happen to me' theory, forms the very core of becoming vulnerable and a potential victim.

Emergency and Survival Preparedness

Too many people do absolutely nothing to prepare themselves or their loved ones to handle an emergency or dangerous situation.

"It just takes too much time and effort and I can't be bothered".

This is a mantra I hear time and time again.

This false conviction combined with fundamental human lethargy is the biggest obstacle many people face and thinking this way gives us the perfect excuse to put off survival preparation until tomorrow. Or in other words 'NEVER'. Until of course something happens, by which time it's often too late. Urban emergency and survival preparedness is more a mental task than a physical one but there is no doubt that you do need to put some effort into your own safety, because when it comes right down to the line there is no one on the planet that is going to look after you as well as you will.

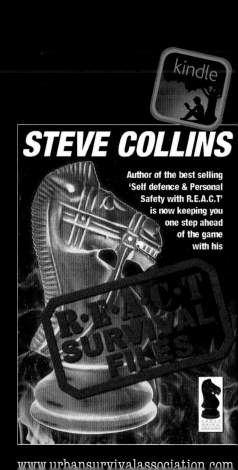

Situation Awareness

**Just a mantra or
crucially valuable tactic ?**

Lecturing on the dangers of firearms
and weapons related crime and
terrorism at the UK Home Office
Police Search Advisers Conference.

An awareness of your surroundings and location is the cornerstone of good security. Situational Awareness is the ability to identify, process, and comprehend information about how to survive in an emergency situation. More simply, it is knowing and understanding what is going on around you.

I have extolled the virtues of 'Situation Awareness' in my writings and training for decades and I have seen the phrase slowly but surely enter the security trainer's glossary. Situation awareness is recognising potentially dangerous environments, but be aware that some of the most peaceful-looking locations can still be affected by crime. Nowhere should be thought of as being completely safe.

Some truly understand the term 'Situation Awareness' but for others it's just a throwaway line with no real substance or understanding of what it means.

The term 'Situation Awareness', owes its birth to the very steep learning curve experienced by the UK in their war against terrorists, both Republican and Loyalist, in Northern Ireland and on the British mainland. As with all counter insurgency situations survival lessons have be learnt quicker than the terrorists learn theirs. Staying ahead of the insurgent's tactical learning curve means keeping friendly forces alive long enough to slow the enemy successes. And of course this has never been truer than it is in today's terrorists' fraught world.

From a personal standpoint, it is much easier to stay out of trouble than it is to get out of trouble. One of the best ways to stay out of trouble is to keep away from the sort of places it is likely to happen. If you are ignorant of your environment and believe "it will never happen to me", you may as well walk around with a great big neon sign saying 'victim'.

The most effective aspect of Situational Awareness involves the ability to project the future actions of elements around you.

After you have been able to identify elements in your environment and can comprehend the situation, it is time to take your Situational Awareness one step further. Use this information to think ahead and determine how it will affect future actions and events in the environment.

Those absorbed in facing a competent and experienced military enemy, or even a run of the mill criminal element must develop training tactics that are vital and rational. However, sadly whether our guardians are in the military, law enforcement, government security, or in the private security sector, training is always budget lead and resource sensitive. Even those with substantial budgets struggle with the needs of those on the front line.

All physical skills need hands on training and regular practice and refreshers, however I believe an understanding of 'Situation Awareness' is a means that addresses the inability of operational personnel to regularly retrain and refresh.

There is a saying... "it is impossible to protect everyone, everywhere all the time from everything". This maxim has never been truer than it is now in 2019.

A large part of the protective remit is to understand risk and that high risk situations are arduous and adrenaline demanding and draining to the body. Intensive concentration is exhausting and in most cases a high state of awareness cannot be maintained for periods of hours let alone days, without a serious degradation of effectiveness.

The genuine protection professional needs to be able to understand when to 'up their game' and equally 'when it's safe to relax'. To achieve this ultimate and enviable mental state is the goal of understanding 'Situation Awareness'.

The skills required to effectively protect those at risk such as shooting, driving, intelligence gathering, surveillance and first aid are all secondary to understanding how to become, and stay situationally aware. All of the physical skills are of course critical in the reactive stage of an operation. However the best kind of skill will allow the protection professional to avoid having to find out whether or not their shooting and driving skills are up to scratch. 'Situation Awareness' will teach you to avoid danger.

Truly understanding 'Situation Awareness' will dramatically reduce the need for using physical fighting skills.

Furthermore 'Situation Awareness' can be constantly practiced, tested and modified in any operational situation and is truly sustainable whereas training and re training is all too often not sustainable.

I asked the question, is 'Situation Awareness' just a mantra or crucially valuable tactic? You can make up your own mind with regards to that.

"Defending Yourself and Drowning Amount to the Same Thing"

If you were drowning, the only thing you would desire is to breathe. Every cell in your body would scream out from the depths of your very soul to be allowed to breathe cool fresh air back into your lungs once more. You would fight like a tiger to overcome any obstacle that got in the way of you reaching the surface, and you would clutch at any straw if you thought it was going to save you from the abyss.

If you are faced with a violent life threatening predator, the only way you will successfully defend yourself is if you have the same resolve as you would if you were drowning.

If you have a critical need to defend yourself and you fight to survive with the same ferocity as a drowning man fighting for air....then you will defend yourself effectively.

Ask yourself one simple question...

HOW MUCH DO YOU WANT TO BREATHE?

Dedicated to all law enforcement officers throughout the world, who have been killed or maimed in the line of duty.

Every day the law enforcement community worldwide is imperilled by the nature of their chosen profession. The risks become all too apparent when attention is drawn to yet another police officer's death. As there is no single profile of any criminal and, therefore, one cannot assume that only certain types of people carry weapons, any situation that officers face can put them in critical danger. Tragic circumstances can result from a basic lack of weapons awareness training, ignoring standard operational procedures, misunderstanding of the phrase 'presumed compliance' or just the deadly combination of a particular type of police officer and a particular type of offender. All these points highlight a continuing need for more comprehensive and in-depth training.

As we are all acutely aware, over 3000 innocent people died on September 11th 2001. One major contributing factor was lack of training and in particular, lack of weapons awareness training. You see it makes absolutely no difference whatsoever how much sophisticated state-of-the-art detection equipment is at your disposal, if you don't know what the weapons you're searching for look like, you won't find them! And since 9/11, not detecting disguised and concealed weapons doesn't bear thinking about.

You, as police officers on the streets of our cities, face these potentially deadly threats every single day. A key, a cigarette package, a lipstick, a watch, a comb, even a gum wrapper are amongst the literally hundreds of common, everyday items which have been used, converted or adapted into concealed and deadly weapons. That innocuous-looking watch could just mean your time is up, that ordinary pen could be used to write your death warrant. If you don't assume that every personal item on a suspect hides a potentially lethal device, you could end up dead from what you thought was a piece of 'Juicy Fruit' gum. A lack of basic training in weapon's awareness and recognition could kill you and the people in your care.

It is actually the very ordinariness of some of these weapons that makes them so lethal. Disguised, improvised, adapted, converted, commercially manufactured or homemade; they pose a deadly threat to us all. As I have said, they often look nothing like weapons. In fact, the design and concealment of a weapon is only limited by an individual's imagination. In my book 'The Manual of Prohibited and Concealable Weapons', we show almost a thousand images of different types of weapons, their use and methods of their concealment. Some are unmistakable - they look exactly like weapons, but a significant number look like anything but weapons.

The overriding principle is simple and should form the nucleus of all weapons' awareness and detection training. If it looks like a gun it is a gun, if it looks like a knife it's probably a knife and if it looks like a bomb there's a good chance it's a bomb. Simple enough, but the point is, if you only look for the obvious things, those are the only things you'll ever find. It is imperative that all law enforcement officers are trained to look more closely at the innocuous-looking items - pens, mobile phones, cigarette lighters, rings, matchboxes, combs and brushes, belts, credit cards etc.

In fact, all the things that definitely don't look like weapons are just the things that should be scrutinized. In other words, don't trust anything - they could all be weapons of one kind or another. Always assume that they are. Guilty until proven innocent should be the rule. There are little old Grandmothers out there capable of killing you with what's in their purse!

Firearms

Let's look at firearms first. Every three-year-old kid knows what a gun looks like. Sadly however, very few law enforcement officers or security professionals know what guns can be made to look like. Gun manufacturers, particularly those in Eastern Europe, seem to be devising more and more firearms that are particularly difficult to recognize and, therefore, detect. Guns built to look like mobile phones, key-ring fobs, signet rings, pens, screwdrivers, penknives, cigarette lighters, belt buckles and even cigarette packets are all out there. Many have been specifically designed to defeat security. They have all been designed to deceive and kill. Commercially manufactured guns are one thing; homemade and improvised are another. They are all just as lethal as their professionally-made cousins. Some are extremely crude in design and manufacture, and the users often run the risk of blowing their own fingers off. However, many are very well made and are becoming increasingly more sophisticated.

Some firearms are conversions, some are re-activated and some have even been adapted from kid's toys. Today's treacherous criminals are more inventive than ever before and will go to great lengths to acquire or fashion their own homemade firearms. Unfortunately, in my experience the vast majority of professional security personnel and police officers are blissfully unaware that these disguised guns even exist, or just how small a firearm can actually be. I am, at present, engaged in the preparation of an international disguised and adapted firearms initiative with the UK National Criminal Intelligence Service and Interpol, to try and address some of these awareness problems.

Knives.

Not Rambo! Not the carving knife out of the kitchen drawer! Lethal as they are, we all know what they look like - you're not going to easily conceal one or smuggle it through a security check. However, edged weapons are, without question, amongst the easiest of all weapons to conceal. Criminals have always known that the thought of being slashed or stabbed creates more physical and psychological terror than being shot. This is why the blade has often been the preferred weapon of the armed robber and, as recent events have shown, even the smallest and most innocuous knives, such as box-cutters, have caused mass destruction on an horrific scale.

Contrary to popular belief, a knife does not have to be over three inches long to be lethal. It doesn't even have to have a point and it definitely needn't be made of steel. I have studied examples of disguised knives with blades no more than ½ inch long, which will kill just as efficiently as any 8-inch stiletto. Homemade and improvised edged weapons can be amongst the most dangerous. Why? Because they don't look like a weapon! For example, super-glue a razor blade onto the back of a credit card with just a fraction of an inch protruding over the edge. It will nestle in your wallet quite innocently with the rest of your credit cards and yet is capable of slitting someone's throat from ear to ear! The chances are you could still walk onto any aircraft in the world with this type of weapon, unchallenged, although security will probably have relieved you of your nail clippers - a sobering thought.

What did I say earlier? "Look for the obvious and that's what you'll find". Just as with firearms, there are also many examples of commercially manufactured, disguised blades. Staying with the credit card theme for a moment, in December last year some members of the media smuggled several edged weapons on board an aircraft traveling from a major UK airport. One of the items was a little beauty called the Spydercard; a very slim, credit-card-sized, folding lock knife. It is highly concealable, incredibly sharp and capable of being opened very quickly with one hand. Knives like these have been around for years, and not just the Spydercard. Knives such as the vicious razor-like Tekan Security Card and the Tool Logic Credit Card Companion, which conceals a formidable spear-point, serrated push-dagger. Knives like these are sitting in wallets and purses all over the world. How many police officers and security personnel are still unable to recognize and detect these items and could pay the ultimate price, through an abject lack of knowledge and training? With the proliferation of modern, stylish clothing accessories and personal carry-bags such as backpacks and bum-bags (fanny-packs), vicious criminals have even more places in which to conceal lethal weapons.

Many examples of awesome-looking knives are manufactured and sold for the purpose of personal protection. Although the vast majority are made of traditional materials, there are many that are manufactured in high impact plastic or a glass-reinforced nylon called Zytel. Some are even moulded to look like hairbrushes and yet they are all capable of inflicting just as much damage as any steel blade. With names such as The Cat, Ace of Spades, Delta Dart and the CIA letter opener, plastic and Zytel weapons pose a major threat to you.

Cigarette lighters are so common in all our lives, we almost don't notice them. Unfortunately, Europe is overrun with ordinary-looking, fully functional cigarette lighters that hold a nasty little secret. Automatic switch-blades. Yes, you can light someone's cigarette and stab them in the eye at the same time! Nice. The point is, if you can hide a flick-knife in a lighter, you can hide a blade in anything; pens, lipsticks, belt buckles, key fobs, coins, jewellery – is that a crucifix or a dagger? It might be both! Only recently, a major UK police force identified a vicious and highly concealable edged weapon adapted from a wire coat hanger. If you know they exist, you have more chance of detecting them and therefore surviving them.

The answer is training, training and more training, and police officers around the world deserve the best training available to ensure that their predecessors have not died in vain.

Tools of

he trade

Nearest Target, Nearest Weapon

A simple way of utilising your body's natural weapons

Never ever punch with a clenched fist. Why? Because "punches break hands not heads". Sustaining sprained, dislocated and broken fingers is not a good way to start defending yourself.

Always think in terms of open hands. Slaps, rakes and finger jabs are much more effective and versatile than punches. If you must clench your fist use the side of your hand like a hammer.

Using the principle of nearest target, nearest weapon eliminates the problem and tactical dilemma of 'what to do next'. Being encumbered with too many choices slows you down, therefore, no matter what position you are in, you will have a natural weapon at your disposal, directly in line with a target on your assailants body. Hit it! Grab it! Kick it! Bite it! Pinch it! Tear it! It doesn't matter what it is, just go for it.

Eyes, ears, neck, fingers, groin even a big toe - if that is your nearest target, attack it. (You do not need a **black belt** to understand this principle).

63

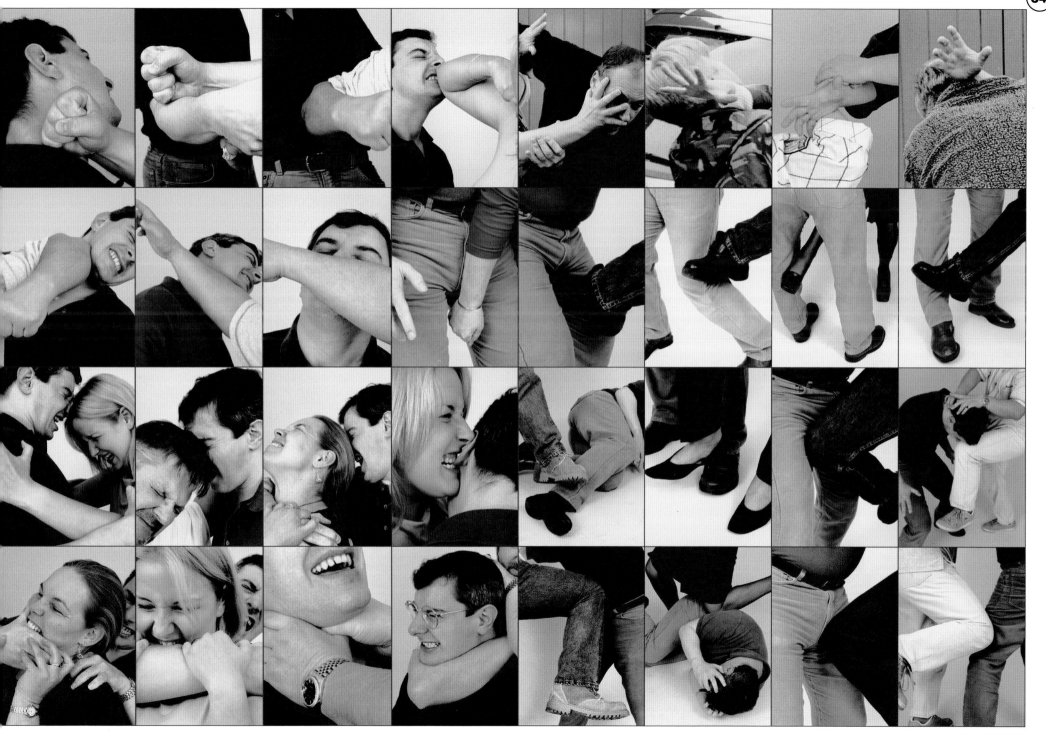

Sweat more when you train,

bleed less when you fight

"Ones Hands should be the cutting edge of the Mind"

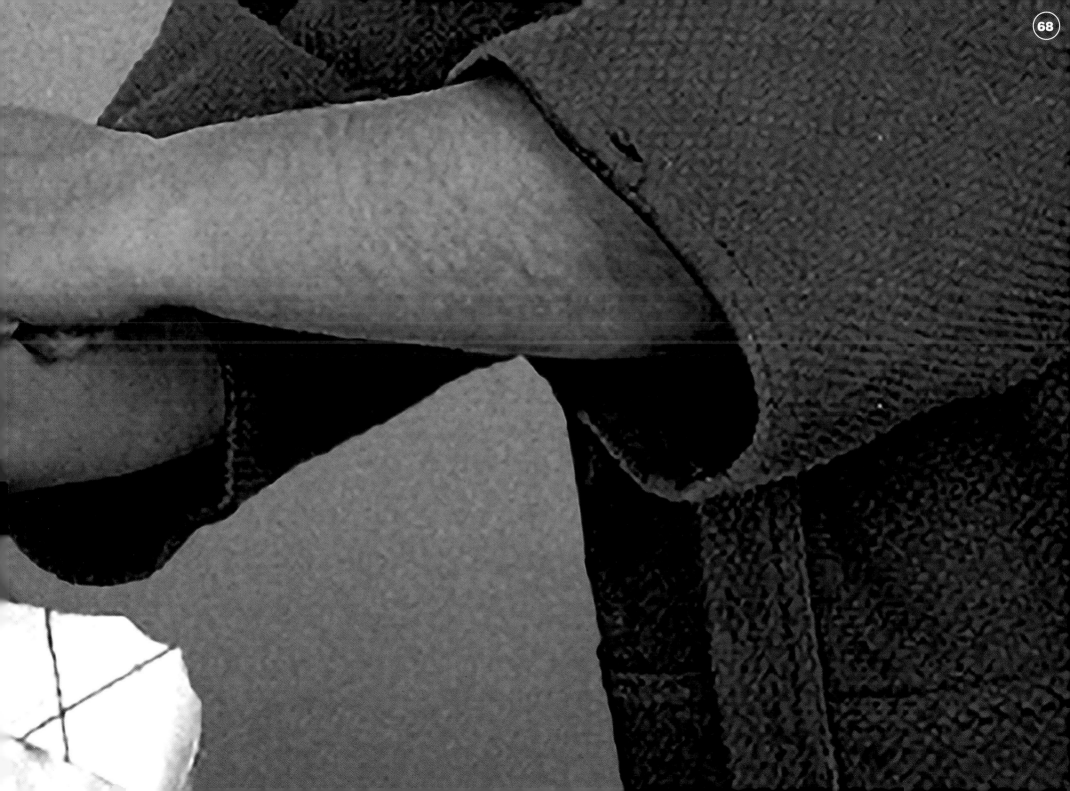

Strategy is the Way of the warrior.

If a warrior attains the true virtue of strategy, that man
can defeat ten men, and so a hundred men can defeat a thousand, and a thousand
can defeat ten thousand. In my strategy, one man is the same as ten thousand men.

If there is a Way involving the spirit of not being defeated, protecting oneself and gaining honour, it is the
Way of Strategy.

If a man knows and understands Strategy, he will see it in everything.

From the 'Go Rin No Sho' (Book of Five Rings) by Miyamoto Musashi 1584 - 1645

THE REACT-OR

After years of painstaking study and research into the history and use of small close quarter hand-held combat tested weapons, I conceived and designed the REACT-OR.

Thousands of hours of study and training culminated in the creation of a device solely designed as a less-than-lethal, close quarter compliance tool.

There lies at the heart of the REACT-OR's design an ethos that bestows it with a long and prestigious pedigree. My inspiration was the Buddhist religious icon and weapon, known as a Vajra, meaning 'thunderbolt'.

I created the REACT-OR specifically to bridge the gap that presently exists between the lethal and less-than-lethal technology currently available to law enforcement agencies.

Deborah demonstrating the awesome power of the REACT-OR. Debs was my business partner for almost 30 years, but sadly passed away in 2010.
She was the best female R.E.A.C.T trainer there ever was.

Throughout the history of close quarter combat, every system in the world has its roots embedded in the use of a weapon or weapons of some description. My R.E.A.C.T System is no exception to this rule.

Although R.E.A.C.T is a personal protection awareness system that teaches the practitioner to avoid confrontation and violence wherever possible, the system recognises that sometimes it may be necessary for the professional to resort to the use of an appropriate weapon.

The REACT-OR is the R.E.A.C.T System's own close quarter compliance tool for those situations when the use of a firearm or other weapon is not appropriate or readily available, but an equaliser is required.

The REACT-OR is Total Control at your fingertips.

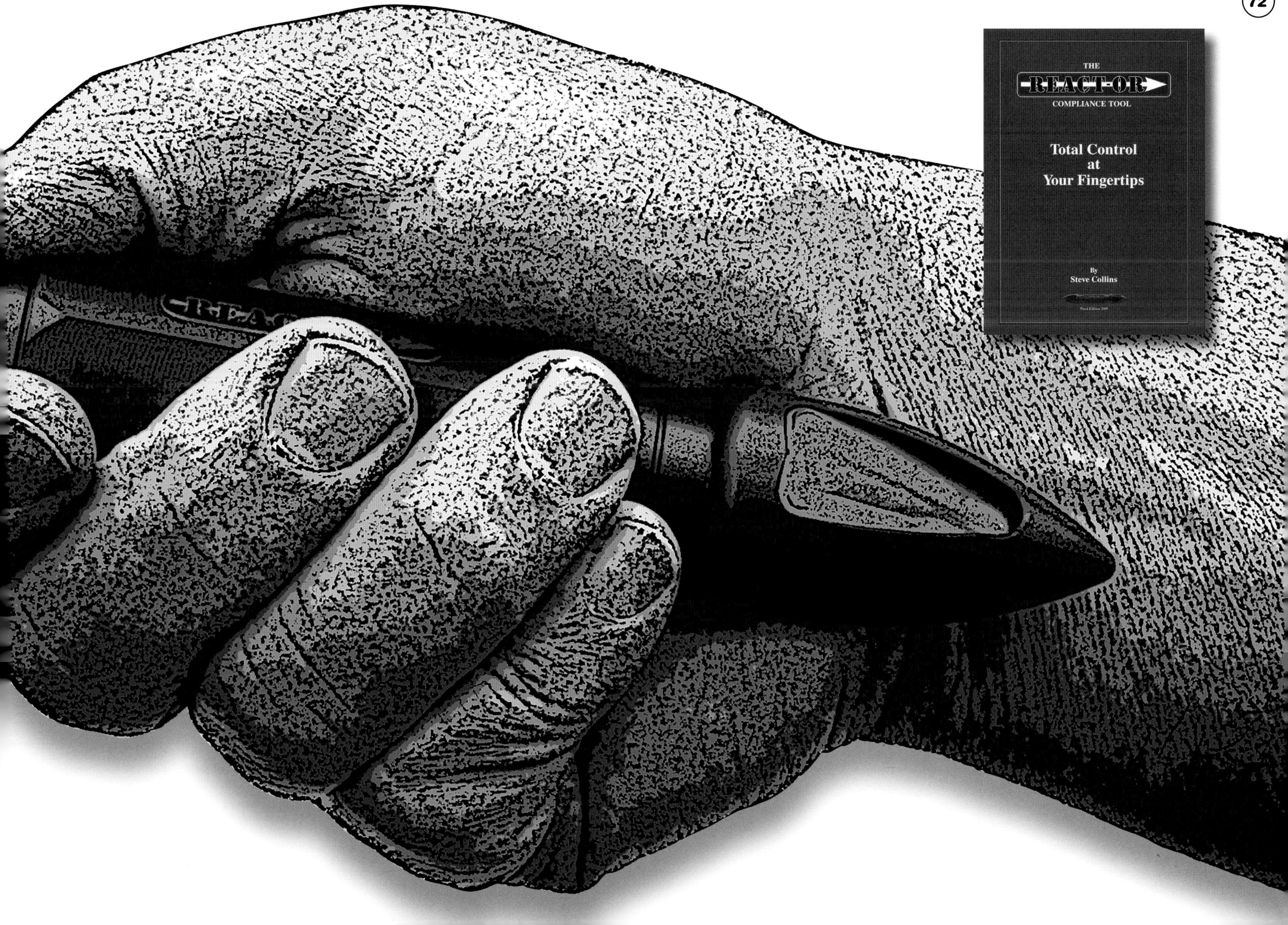

THE

REACT-OR ►

COMPLIANCE TOOL

**Total Control
at
Your Fingertips**

By
Steve Collins

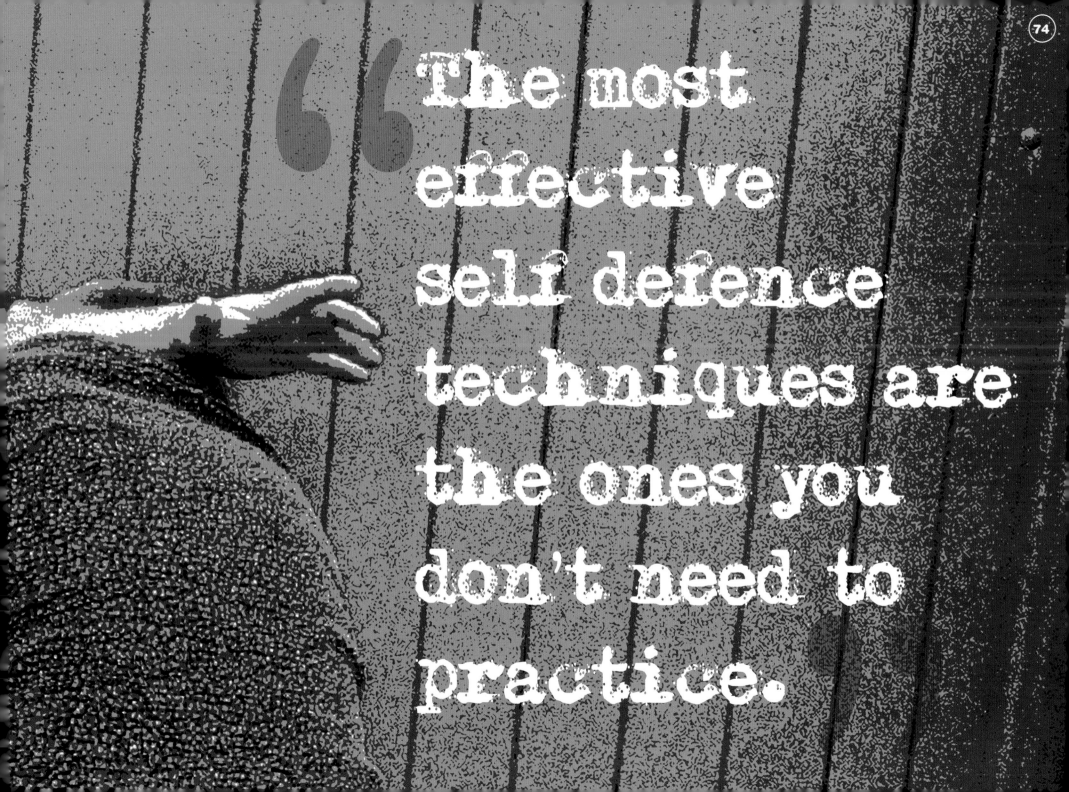

"The most effective self defence techniques are the ones you don't need to practice.

"Control the structure, control the man"

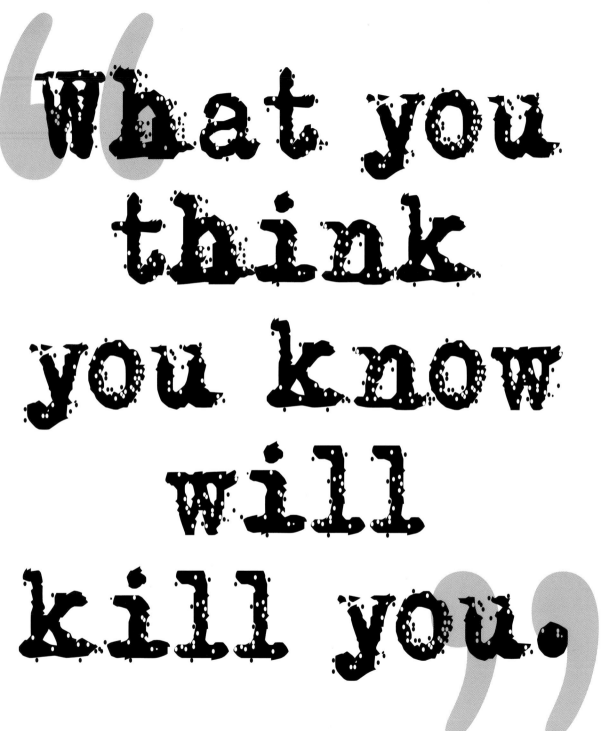

What you think you know will kill you.

Victims of violent crime often say that it seemed as if it came out of nowhere. The fact is that's hardly ever true, there will have been plenty of warning, and plenty of opportunity to recognize and evaluate the danger signs in advance, but sadly most of the time the victim didn't see them, ignored them, or just didn't recognize their significance.

There is a common saying among personal safety teachers: "What you think you know will kill you". Meaning that familiarity often blinds us to the significance of the signals of pending danger. What you "think" you know about violent crime could blind you to the importance of the warning signs. In my R.E.A.C.T System we talk about 'Recognising the Threat', and there are a set of simple and obvious stages to help you do this. These stages are inherent in the development of a violent crime. If you are aware of this process you will see that they are predictable and quite recognizable. Understanding these stages will enable you to spot and react to danger in advance.

There has to be a build-up to an act of violence.

Criminals are not generally speaking sitting in front of the TV with a nice cup of coffee and a jam doughnut then suddenly leaping up and attacking someone. As human beings the act of actually committing a violent crime requires us to go through a set process that takes time to develop. Even the most violent of people are not normally capable of instantaneously becoming violent; they need time to go through a set of recognizable physiological and psychological changes in order to attack someone physically. Only in cases of severe and extreme mental instability, as found on a mental ward, will a person be capable of erupting instantly into violence.

Any person who is preparing to attack you physically will give off certain signals. Their body will literally betray their intent. People who have been assaulted often say, "I knew there was something wrong but I just couldn't put my finger on it". As I said earlier, the victim didn't see the signs, ignored them, or just didn't recognize their significance. The first letter in my R.E.A.C.T System is R for Recognise and the first step of the journey to understanding what danger looks like.

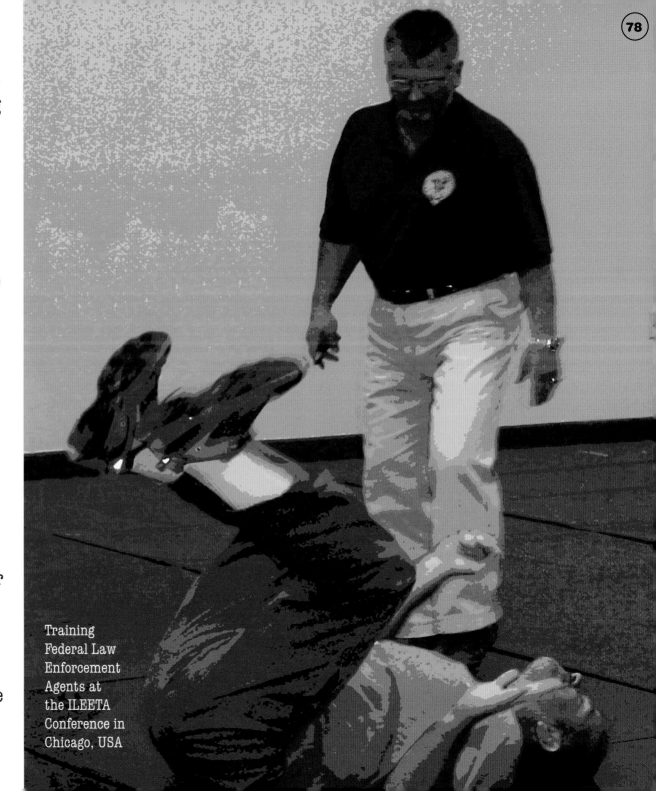

Training
Federal Law
Enforcement
Agents at
the ILEETA
Conference in
Chicago, USA

My good friend, defensive tactics instructor, Tony Blauer, created the SPEAR System (Spontaneous Protection Enabling Accelerated Response); utilising the bodies natural 'flinch response' to danger. As I have previously said, the most effective techniques are those you don't need to practice.

"Turn a natural action into a combative tactic"

Don't mess with the SAS

Some random stills I have dug out of the archives from about 1995.
They are from a film shoot on Self Defence I made with one of my best mates and work colleagues 'Yorky C'.
Mr. C was a long serving soldier with the 22nd Special Air Service (SAS).

Sadly, I can't find any traces of the original film, but these stills remind me of just how real we tried to make it.

I can still feel the sickening thud as Yorky slammed my head into that steel roller shutter door.

Bless him....Big bully!!

"Intent is always in the eyes"

Are kids becoming more violent because of adults?

Sadly street crime and violence has permeated the very fabric of our lives. In our inner cities, suburban areas and now even small country villages no-one seems to be immune. Violence degrades the quality of all our lives. This diminished quality of life ranges from an inability to walk safely alone in the park or on the streets of our own towns, to the forced installation of expensive security systems and, because of an abject lack of a police presence, the necessity to formulate neighbourhood watch groups. Even in our quietest country villages long gone are the days when front doors were left open so friends and neighbours could just pop in.

Reports of children committing suicide as a result of experiencing violence and bullying in schools are rife. Children carrying weapons and committing horrific crimes of violence, murder and rape are on the increase. Many youths simply believe that they have to carry a weapon at school and on the streets in order to protect themselves. All these things are growing to epidemic proportions so much so that there is now a worldwide problem with aggressive and violent behaviour from children and adolescents not only on the streets of our cities, but in our small towns and rural villages. Bizarre as it may sound, some communities are literally living in fear of the local kids.

For many years there has been huge amounts of psychosocial research into violent and aggressive behaviour. This research has shown there to be a substantial link in aggressive behaviour from infancy to adulthood.

A child of 5 or 6 years who shows aggressive and violent behaviour is more likely than others to exhibit delinquent, criminal and violent behaviour in adolescence and adulthood. Simple fact; in the majority of cases violent children grow up into violent adults. However, no child is born violent. There's no such thing as a three-year old mass murderer or serial killer. Yes, very young children have killed and do kill, but many more children are killed by adults than there are adults killed by children. In order for a child to develop into a violent adolescent and consequently a violent adult, the child first has to be exposed to violence and that first exposure will invariably have been at the hands of an older person. As I said earlier, children aren't born violent. True, but children are born into violence and violent situations.

In very simplistic terms (and because child abuse is a deep, dark subject that would certainly need more than this short article to explore) the first and most fundamental cause is to have suffered violent abuse at home at the hands of a parent/parents. However, even if a child is not on the receiving end but regularly witnesses aggressive and violent behaviour being dished out to others by a father, mother or older brothers and sisters, they will and do conclude that violent behaviour is quite acceptable and a normal part of life.

All children learn by modelling and imitation. In other words they copy what they see. Even if a child comes from a perfectly stable non violent home, it's bewildering to think just how many acts of violence that child will have witnessed before the age of twelve. Violence in the media, gratuitous violence at the football ground, the symbolic yet non the less explicit violence in TV shows or at the movies, the death and mutilation glamorised in hi-tec interactive video games, not to mention the violence and abuse advocated in modern rock and rap music, especially towards women. Consuming vast quantities of violent material plus the likelihood of actually having to live in a violent environment, add to the mix the fact that many of these kids (for of course that's all they are) have been conditioned into believing that resorting to violence is perfectly acceptable in order to get what they want. This plus an unshakeable belief that the more aggressive and violent they are the more 'respect' they will command and you have a serious problem. A problem that touches us all.

In the majority of cases where children have been violent to or even killed their parents it has been found that the child has usually been abused in some manner - degraded, humiliated, beaten, sexually abused or even tortured. The child often responds to violence with violence, for that's all it understands. Sometimes an abused child can turn its violent anger towards a sibling within the family.

Most people are afraid of gangs of rowdy juveniles and at times with good reason. However, as with rape victims, the majority of people attacked and killed by adolescents are known to them. If a stranger is killed it is usually during a robbery. This sometimes happens because the juvenile will panic, but it's more likely simply because of peer pressure, and usually from older kids. Statistics show that murder is more likely to occur when two or more juveniles jointly commit a crime. Also, if they are under the influence of alcohol or drugs, the more aggressive and violent they are likely to be. So staying away from gangs of drunken teenagers would seem a sensible thing to do.

In reality violent crime touches us all in one way or another therefore we have all become victims of violent crime. Even if it has never happened to you personally, the likelihood is that it will happen to someone you know - a friend, neighbour or even a relation and even if that's not the case, the fact that we are forced to witness almost every day on the TV and in the newspapers the misery and suffering inflicted on total strangers by violent crime, gives us all cause for concern about our own safety and that of our loved ones. So you see, we are all victims by the very thought of aggressive and violent behaviour.

Anyone who has experienced a violent tragedy in their lives will know how they were forced to take a long hard look at everything in their lives from that day on. Often a long and arduous search for responsibility engulfs the mind, but the results are usually unrewarding. People related to a victim tend to fall into two categories - those who blame themselves and those who blame others.

'THE GIFT OF FEAR'
In Gavin De Becker's book 'THE GIFT OF FEAR' De Becker writes of one Willie Bosket acquiring remarkable criminal credentials very early in life. Apparently by the time he was fifteen this young man had stabbed twenty-five people and been in and out of detention facilities for an estimated two thousand other crimes. He was arrested for killing two people and commented, "I did it for the experience." But because he was still only a minor he could only be detained for five years. Even behind bars Willie Bosket's violence continued. He allegedly set fire to his cell seven times and violently attacked guards nine times. "I'm a monster the system created," he says. One thing for certain, Willie was not born that way, so someone or something created him. Where should the blame lie for Willie's actions? In the State of New York, USA there is now a legal statute that allows juveniles to be tried as adults. It is called 'The Willie Bosket Law'.

De Becker relates another very poignant story. One brother says to the other, *"Why did you grow up to be a drunk?"* The answer came back,

"Because our dad was a drunk". The second brother then asked,

"Why didn't you grow up to be a drunk?" The answer came back,

"Because our dad was a drunk". Many kids live through awful childhoods and still grow up to become upright, productive, contributing and law-abiding adults. Whatever the outcome, it's adults that make children into whoever they become.

It's not just the UK it's an international problem. For example, panic broke out amongst a crowd on the streets of Berlin. As people were leaving a celebration open-air sound-and-light concert, a knife-wielding teenager went on a rampage and, suddenly began to randomly slash and stab at the people in the crowd; the attacker had mingled with the crowd as they were leaving the show. Over 100 police officers and 11 ambulances were called out, but because of the narrowness of the streets it was difficult for police and emergency services to reach the scene. Although none of his victims had life-threatening injuries this young lad managed to wound 27 people in a very short space of time. Many of the injured were hospitalised. The teenager was as always known to police for previous acts of violence.

Knife attacks, shootings, acid attacks, beating, rapes and terrorism invade our lives and with the exception of BREXIT theses things monopolize the media.

Fact: Violent crime is on the increase.

Fact: Those who commit violent crimes are getting younger.

Fact: We are all victims of violent crime.

Fact: Not enough is being done about it.

Choke or Strangle?

CHOKE

The choke cuts off the air supply to the brain by exerting pressure on the throat and larynx. Choking is a slow and painful journey to unconsciousness or even death. It can take 60 seconds or more for a choke to work and even if death does not occur serious damage to the throat is common.

If you had to defend yourself and in doing so you ended up choking a person to death you would have an immensely difficult job justifying your actions to a judge and jury.

STRANGLE

The strangle applies pressure to both the jugular vein and carotid artery, cutting off the blood supply and oxygen to the brain. Quick and relatively painless, it is possible to render a person unconscious in less than 15 seconds if continuous pressure is applied. If you release the strangle as soon as the person becomes unconscious, a full recovery will be made in a few seconds. However, a carotid restraint is potentially deadly if held on too long, and is guaranteed to be lethal if held for two minutes or more.

know the difference!

"We are all victims of knife crime"

First and foremost let me explain that this is NOT! a "HOW TO DO IT BOOK". You will find no knife fighting techniques within its pages. Nor will you read about yet another realistic and devastatingly effective knife defence system, handed down to me by some ancient master who dwells on the miasma covered mountain tops of the far and mystical east. NO! One reason I wrote this book is because, just like you, I am, and have been, a victim of knife crime. "I've never been a victim of knife crime" I hear you say. Well, I would beg to differ.

Knife attacks are such an unpleasant subject that most of us don't even want to think about it. However, the fact is we are given no choice but to think about it. Knife crime affects each and every one of us. We are all touched by it. Even if you've never been attacked, even if you don't know someone who's been attacked, and even if there's never been a knife attack in your town, you are still indirectly a victim of knife crime. Every week, if not every day, we are bombarded with media coverage of yet another stabbing, another bloody murder; another innocent citizen robbed or raped at knife point, another kid having the life snatched out of them on the way home from school. Retailers have to install extra security measures in order to meet the requirements of their insurers, resulting in the knock-on effect

of higher prices for goods. The list goes on and on. So like it or not, you are, I am and everyone else is a victim of weapons-related crime and especially knives. Every time you go through a security checkpoint you become a victim, every time you stand in line at the airport waiting to be searched you become a victim. In fact every time the subject is forced into your life you are being victimised by it. The mere fact that I thought there was a need to write a book on the subject is confirmation of knife crime victimization.

My work takes me all over the world and by its very nature I am exposed to the causes and aftermath of horrendous weapon-related violence and terrorism.

The horrifying reality is something we cannot afford to ignore. Apathy and denial steals people's lives. Therefore, I make no apologies for some of the language in these pages and no apologies for some of the graphic images I have used. Knife attacks are as real and as deadly as cancer and, sadly, reaching epidemic proportions.

Both my parents passed away with cancer and, over the years, several dear friends have gone the same way. I possessed no knowledge that could have helped them, but I do have knowledge and an understanding of knives and knife attacks, which could help you, and that's why I wrote this book.

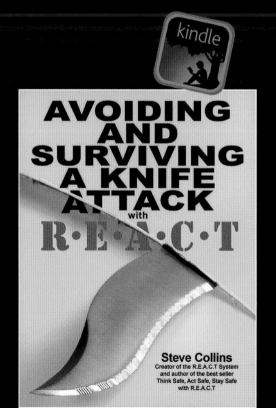

kindle

AVOIDING AND SURVIVING A KNIFE ATTACK with R·E·A·C·T

Steve Collins
Creator of the R.E.A.C.T System
and author of the best seller
Think Safe, Act Safe, Stay Safe
with R.E.A.C.T

"Playing your role..."

Human behaviour often falls into set patterns. We are all, generally speaking, predisposed to act out certain role-plays, almost as if we were reading from a script. An understanding that certain kinds of behaviour will almost certainly trigger responses that can be manipulated and therefore used to your own advantage is a very useful tool. Furthermore, when you realise that the vast majority of people will not even understand why they are responding the way they are, can put you in a very powerful position. It is possible to manipulate a situation without the other person realising what is happening to them, until of course, it's too late.

An example of this type of manipulation is the predator/prey role-play. Most of us are conditioned from being young children to respond to authority in a certain way. We are usually instilled from a very early age with the belief that authority should be respected and therefore, even if we don't like it, we are generally predisposed to comply with it. This conditioning is what the predator relies on. The process of manipulation begins with the predator handing you his script and in a very authoritative manner explains that you are about to co-star in his play. The story line is where he attacks you and, because in the script you are described as 'the helpless victim', your role is to do everything you are told to do. He continues to explain that the story has a happy ending and by following the script to the letter, he gets what he wants and you get to go home unharmed. Not following the script however will result in severe punishment. Most people will follow the script. Why? Simple. It's because the predator has typecast them into the role of victim, and they are being manipulated into a situation that has triggered a predetermined response to comply with authority, especially if the consequences of not doing so will result in some sort of punishment being administered. They are conditioned to believe that once the curtain goes up and the play begins they have reached a point of no return and therefore must continue to act out their role. This is not true! If you can change your role in the play the script will change too.

In this type of confrontation one person has already assumed the role of aggressor/predator. Conventionally the other person is now left with two choices:

1. Frightened and compliant victim.

2. Counter-aggressor.

The predator will be expecting and relying on you playing the frightened and compliant victim role. If you go down this road the predator will act accordingly. He will posture, threaten and intimidate. Showing fear will fuel the fire of his aggression and play to his ego. Statistics show that the likelihood is that he will still harm you regardless of all the promises to the contrary. Begging not to be hurt is a sure fire way to get just the opposite.

Playing the victim role is not the way to get off lightly. More often than not all it means is that it takes a little longer before you get hurt, as well as robbed, raped or even both.

The role of the counter-aggressor is also fraught with danger. If you go back to your own childhood, or even look at your own children taking the role of counter-aggressors with you, it would be considered an act of defiance, insolence or insubordination and dealt with accordingly. The rules are plain and ingrained into us all. Subordinates simply do not answer their superiors back. Remember this is the predator's script, he is the star and his role is a superior one to yours. Now faced with a sudden threat from a counter-aggressor the predator will react in a predetermined manner and his own defensive reflexes will kick in. He will, almost subconsciously, make the decision to attack and probably with extreme violence.

So as you can see neither of these scripts actually has a happy ending. If you are going to change your role and as a consequence the script, you have to do it as far in advance of the curtain going up as you can.

Change The Script And Take Control

Most of us are comfortable when we are following a set pattern. We are in our comfort zone; we know what to do and what's expected from us. If someone or something breaks our pattern and we suddenly find ourselves in unfamiliar territory, we become confused and uncomfortable, as a result we are less natural and what we do and say requires more thought.

Breaking the aggressors set pattern, or in others words changing his script to your script is the key that will help you change your role from prey to predator. The aggressor is locked into a pattern of behaviour that has been predetermined by his script. If you break the script he has to formulate a new response, which means he is forced to stop and think about what to say and do next. This whole process slows the situation down because thinking out a new response is obviously going to take longer than following a set pattern.

This is all well and good, but how do you change his script without becoming the frightened and compliant victim or the counter-aggressor?

1. Don't react at all. Stay calm and just walk by as if he wasn't even there. This isn't in his script, it makes no sense, your supposed to follow his lead and act out your role in the play.

The aggressor will be confused, but only for a second or too. Hopefully, in the time it takes him to amend his script, you will be out of the danger zone and ready to run as fast as your legs will carry you.

2. Act out the cool but ready-for-action role. Simply stand your ground without making any aggressive actions, verbally or physically. Say nothing, just stand and stare with a calm, expressionless face. Training will help you to remain calm under stress, but even with no training you have given him a big problem. This type of response, or in reality lack of it can be very intimidating. It manipulates the situation by giving out a powerful massage saying I don't consider you as anything that I should be getting concerned about.

3. Respond verbally with something totally irrelevant to the situation, non-aggressively with friendly dialogue. Often the best thing is to say something that requires him to think of an answer. Ask a question. "That's a fantastic jacket, where did you get it?"; "What's the time mate I'm in a real hurry?" ; "I'm looking for Benson Drive do you know where it is?" Anything that stops you getting drawn into his script.

Once the pattern is broken a new one must take its place, and this time with you taking the leading role. However, never lose sight of the fact that this person standing in front of you is probably still predisposed to violence. Therefore it is imperative that you use whatever time you have to open a window of opportunity and extract yourself from the situation as quickly as possible. Your action could be as simple as just running away. Or even, but only as a last resort and only if you're sure you have no alternative, launching your own pre-emptive attack. Almost all street predators are cowards, on the lookout for helpless victims. Often they are incapable of tackling someone face-to-face - unless that person is playing out the victim role of course. They're quite happy with the surprise attack from behind, but when faced with a calm and resolute person they are often fazed and unable to continue in the light of the opposition. Ask yourself this simple question: "If a common street robber thought that by attacking you he would probably be injured, restrained and forcibly escorted to a police station, would he still attack you?" Answer, NO! Although that, somewhat idealistic, scenario is never likely to be played out in full, it does illustrate the mind set you should be in and it is the image you should be portraying. Be careful not to give these people any reason to resort to violence and remember, the frightened victim or the counter-aggressor is just the trigger they need. Also, don't fall into the trap of being pushed into making the first move, giving them the excuse to retaliate. You must not provide the trigger, but you must be ready to act as soon as the opportunity presents itself. Make your move when you're ready not when they're ready. Remember, the predator does not want to fight you; he wants to control and intimidate you into following his script. Don't allow yourself to get locked into belligerent exchange, in other words don't let your ego take control as this will inevitably lead to violence. Give the predator the chance to walk away without losing face. Many street robbers, when faced with quiet resolve, have to make a decision about what to do next, and assuming they're not too stupid they will recognise the opportunity to move away from you and on to an easier target.

"LEARN TO CHEAT"

In the vast majority of cases when people are faced with real street violence it's akin to being a virgin in the hands of Casanova...
"They are definitely going to get fucked".

Most of us learn self defence in a sterile environment, we train with consent. However, you won't find the street predator in the local church hall on a Tuesday and Thursday night practising his art. He gets all the training he needs on the street, doing it for real!

He's got a host of nasty, sneaky, dirty tricks up his sleeve that he hasn't just politely practised with a friend, oh no, he has actually used them in anger.

If you are endeavouring to survive a violent attack and have no option other than to fight, you must remember one thing about the bad guy.

In short he is going to CHEAT! Yes that's right cheat.

As with playing cards, it's easy to win if you're the only one cheating, but it becomes considerably harder when everyone else is cheating too.

Violence on the street is a game where everybody should be cheating, and the winner is often the one who is better at it. There are no 'Marquis of Queensbury Rules' on the street and believe me it's not always the toughest, fittest, the fastest or the black belt that wins.

To be candid, the street predator is not going to give you a chance to use all that good stuff you were shown in the gym.

When he drops his bombshell on you, it's going to be at his convenience, and not yours. Because he understands 'getting in first' is the major component that determines who comes out on top.

If you don't recognise the danger and don't understand what it looks like as it develops, then you are going to become just another victim of violent crime, before you have a chance to bring out your best defensive tactics and techniques.

The reality is that the predator you will be facing has experience, it's not a matter of training for him, it's a matter of doing.

As I've already said, the likelihood is that you are that virgin in the clutches of Casanova. He knows what he's doing is a winning strategy because he's done it hundreds of times before.

It doesn't matter how good you are in the Dojo or training hall, survival against habitually violent people has less to do with physical prowess than knowing how to spot when someone is trying to set you up for a sucker punch. Mark my words, once he gets that advantage, he will never let you up and to allow you to unleash all those killer moves that you paid so much to learn.

Your safety is your responsibility, but it's not about learning to fight, it's about having an ace up your sleeve, so learn to cheat!!

false

Fear is often the brain fixating on something that hasn't yet happened and it's always negative. Fear management is the key to handling all situations.

In my REACT System I use the word FEAR as an acronym: 'False Evidence Appearing Real' to try and explain my beliefs about the emotion we all know as FEAR and how the phrase can be used as a fear management tool.

Fear is a part of life. Fear is a warning mechanism. Fear's job is to help you survive, not cripple you into being unable to function. It is possible to be totally paralysed with fear. Think of a rabbit caught in a car's headlights. Fear is a perfectly natural, emotional state of mind, just like anger or sorrow. Without it we would all put ourselves in positions of extreme danger all the time and, as a result, probably not live to a ripe old age. Those who say that they are not frightened of anything are either plain liars, deluding themselves or simply particularly stupid. Most of us will think of fear as a negative and, if not understood and managed, it can be devastating. If you allow fear to terrorise you it will control your actions.

False Evidence Appearing Real is a very smart and catchy acronym, but is it true? Some say not. They will argue that calling fear False Evidence is saying that fear is an illusion or a lie. Yes we can create fear as a reaction to believing illusions, lies, or false evidence, and it is true that unhealthy fear is not an illusion. Being afraid is real enough when you are paralysed and unable to function because of it.

An attacker is relying on your fear of them to create confusion and panic and therefore diminish the effectiveness of your response. Fear is an emotion that can cause some of us to act more violently than we

Evidence Appearing Real

would normally and that can have sad consequences. We all have fears, many of them irrational, but nevertheless very, very real to those who have them, such as fear of snakes, spiders, heights, the dentist and so on. What may seem stupid to one person, to another it is a real problem. However, if faced with a potentially violent or confrontational situation, you must try to understand that the feeling of fear is actually a positive emotion. Fear is a natural response to danger, but it can also be self-created, such as the fear of failure, being out of control, being different or being lonely. There is a fear of the future and of death. You may fear love because you fear being rejected; fear being generous because you fear you will not have enough; fear of sharing your thoughts or feelings in case you appear wrong; and fear trusting because you are dominated by self-doubt and insecurity. There is no freedom like that which comes from letting go of fear. This freedom allows you to see the situation with clarity. Suddenly, the worst case scenario isn't so scary after all.

Fear in fact is the memory of danger. It serves a purpose, often keeping us out of danger such as not touching a white hot iron bar, but it is in fact a bit of a fossil. The fight or flight response of fear is a throwback from prehistoric times. Modern life does not hold the same dangers as it did then, and yet our brains still holds the same capacity for fear. Our not so easy quest is to divide healthy fear from unhealthy fear. Healthy fear is what gets you out of the path of a charging bull, or makes you go to the doctor when you know something is not as it should be. Unhealthy fear is where our acronym comes in to play. Evidence that appears to be very real at the time but is mostly a fabrication of the ancient mammalian and reptilian parts of our brain and that part of our human character that wants to keep us imprisoned in our own mind, unwilling to venture out because it's too risky and fraught with danger.

I believe an understanding of the term False Evidence Appearing Real is the key to overcoming unhealthy fear, and as a fear management tool can also help to develop an inner security that will put external threats into a new perspective and the realisation that fear can be your friend. Embrace it, fully experience it, name it, get to know it and make it work for you and not against you. Embrace the fear and recognise that the feelings you are experiencing, both mentally and physically, are your friends and will help you. Fear activates a survival mechanism in us all.

When you are frightened the adrenaline glands dump a cocktail of hormones into the bloodstream, which summons up reserves of power and strength. Your muscles tense in order to ward off an attack, your breathing rate will rapidly increase to supply more oxygen to your body, your heart rate increases to supply more blood to your muscles and you will break out in a cold sweat which has the effect of cooling the body but warming the muscles ready for action. So, while you are feeling like shit, and wanting to throw up, your body is saying, "Come on then, I'm ready to fight!" Make the most of what nature has given you. Fear is your friend. You must breathe through the rush of adrenaline that surges through your system. Focus your mind and co-ordinate the energy. Don't be put off by the fact that you feel bad, you feel apprehensive, your mouth is dry, you may start to tremble and your voice may become broken and high pitched, because these are all natural responses to the situation. You must work through them. Remember, the things you feel are the results of chemicals being released into your system. Yes, you are frightened, but it's OK to be scared. Just try to put it into perspective. You may think of fear as a negative, but, the opposite is the case, fear is actually a positive emotion, if you understand what's happening to you. Unhealthy fear is 'False Evidence Appearing Real' and healthy fear is your friend.

"Coming to terms with violence"

Understanding and coming to terms with the monumental increases in violence that seem to threaten us all is a task too gigantic even to contemplate. There are times when it seems almost impossible to escape the impact of violence on our daily lives. In one way or another it touches us all and in doing so turns us all in to victims.

Many of us, myself included, who inhabit today's modern towns and cities, go about our daily business with underlying concerns about our physical safety. However, our worries tend not to focus on whether or not we are going to become the victim of some terrible mishap like getting knocked down by a bus or hit by some object falling from a roof. No, on the contrary, sadly many people nowadays are anxious about street crime, weapons and terrorism. Law-abiding citizens more often than not look to the police to guard them against such possibilities.

Unfortunately, Police officers cannot be everywhere and even if they could, the reality is that they probably haven't been given sufficient training to enable them to subdue a vicious knife welding mugger and look after someone else at the same time. Even so, people do need to see not just more police officers on our streets, but others in uniform who can offer some form of peace of mind. There is a visibility gap and it's growing, but please remember the Police are not there to look after you, that is your job.

The simple facts are and always have been, that wherever you find issues relating to politics, religion, drugs, sex, or alcohol you will find crime, wherever you find crime you find violence and wherever you find violence you will find guns, bombs, knives and sadly in recent years acid. It is simple, the more crime, the more violence and the more violence the more weapons.

As the diameter of this vicious circle ever widens it becomes increasingly more obvious that if the law will not allow us to protect ourselves, we need more trained people to protect us and of course we all know that's not going to happen.

If you accept the theory that it only takes a small amount of violent criminals to create a huge amount of violent crime, you also have to accept the fact that we need to do more than we are doing to fight against it. And why? Because politics, religion, drugs, sex and alcohol are never going to go away and therefore, nor is violent crime.

It's all too easy to say that it's the government's responsibility or that the police should be doing more. I believe the more knowledge and understanding you have about a threat, the safer you are from it.

Furthermore, we all have a responsibility to do whatever we can to look after ourselves, our loved ones and those in our care, because, believe me, if you don't nobody else will.

"When there is a need for skill, there is no place for brute force."

The Colours

The brain is split into two halves.
The logical left hemisphere and the creative right hemisphere

# of my mind"

For as long as I can remember original ideas and quirky thoughts have continuously whirled through the recesses of my mind - a myriad of colours formed a rich tapestry of ideas, deductions and conclusions which enabled me to forge a career as a professional designer and writer.

The following 5 spreads illustrate just a small number of the favourite thoughts and maxims that I have coined over many years and used in my personal safety training and writing. I call these thoughts 'The colours of my mind' and when my mind is open and receptive the colours are so much more intense and bright.

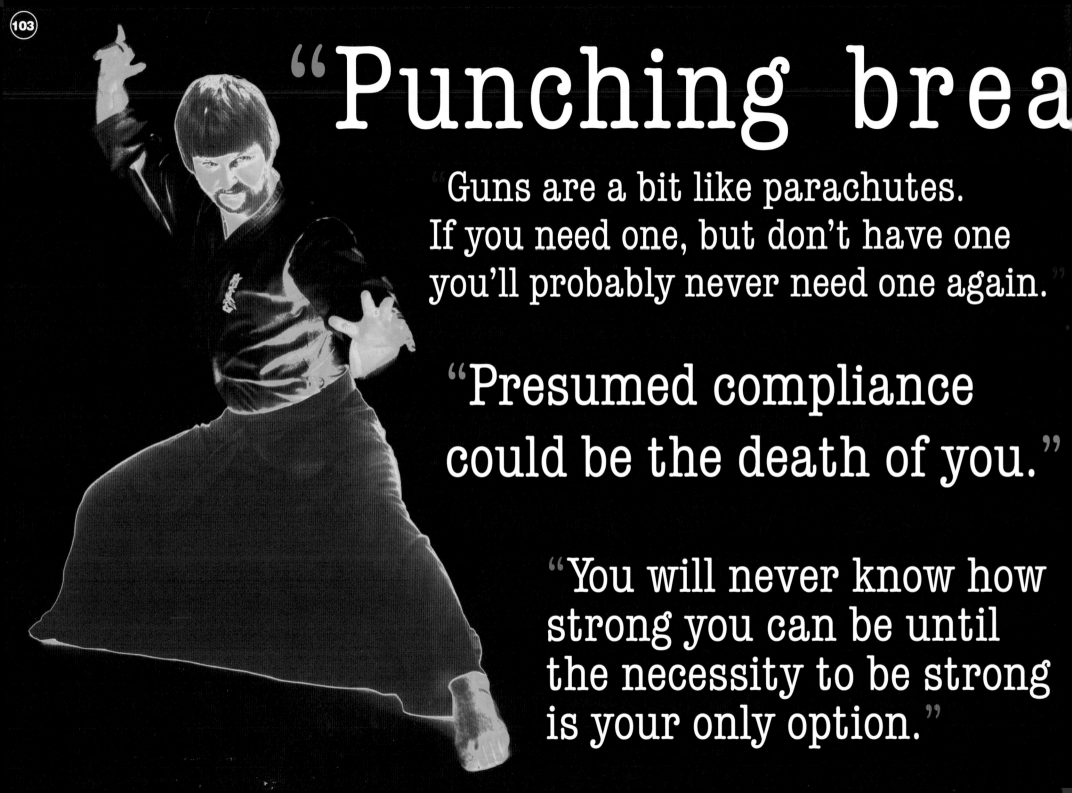

"Punching brea

"Guns are a bit like parachutes. If you need one, but don't have one you'll probably never need one again."

"Presumed compliance could be the death of you."

"You will never know how strong you can be until the necessity to be strong is your only option."

ks hands not heads"

"If they can't see you they can't find you to harm you. If they can't breathe they're not capable of harming you. If they're in agony they are not thinking of harming you and if they can't walk they can't catch you to harm you... what more do you need to know?"

"Awareness is the cornerstone of good personal protection."

"Protect yourself with your intellect if you can, your hands if you have to, but never with your ego."

"STRATEGIES win

"There are only 3 choices 'Give in – Give up – or Give it all you've got"

"All the water on the planet cannot sink a ship unless it gets inside it, so don't let fear and negativity get inside you"

"Never lose sight of your own vulnerability"

"Do not let people mistake your silence for ignorance, your calmness for acceptance or your politeness for weakness"

ights, not TECHNIQUES"

"Do not be ruled by adrenaline, harness it and use it to your advantage"

"As far as Self-Defence is concerned there are only two very simple things to remember..

a. Your safety is 100% your responsibility.

b. Nobody is coming to rescue you"

"You will only defeat an opponent if your desire to win is greater than your fear of defeat"

"There is nothing wrong with getting knocked down, it's not getting back up again that's wrong"

"It is impossible to commit physically if you are not committed mentally"

"Remember, at any given time you have the power to say 'This is not how this story is going to end'"

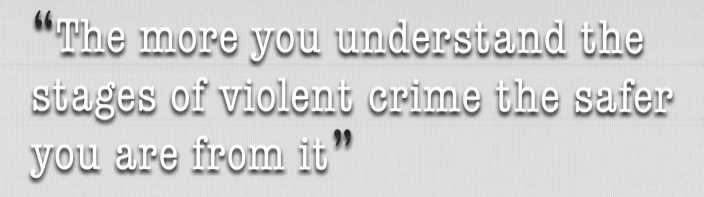

"The more you understand the stages of violent crime the safer you are from it"

"Self defence

"You must make a vow to yourself that your life and the lives of your loved ones is worth fighting for"

"Use your head, before somebody else does"

"Many are defeated, because they lack the courage to run away"

"Defend yourself, because no one else will"

"LOVE me and I will always be in your heart, HATE me and I will always be in your head. So, therefore, I can't lose"

needs no apology"

"You must give yourself permission to take control and become the predator not the prey"

"You can 'get up' or you 'can give up', but if you give up you may never get up again"

"Fear activates our survival mechanism, harness its power"

"R.E.A.C.T is a

"Nobody ever won a fight by standing still"

"There is nothing gentler than real strength"

"Endurance is about the only thing you cannot fake"

"If you can perceive power you can achieve power"

"FEAR-False. Evidence. Appearing. Real.

Don't believe everything you think"

vehicle not a road"

"Everyone has a plan until they get punched in the face"

"Good self defence tactics should make an assailant feel like they've just been hit by a truck they didn't see coming"

"Focus all your physical and mental energy at one point"

"If 50% of your self-defence training results in no practical or effective application then 50% of your training time is wasted"

"You can be a victim or not, the choice is always yours"

"Age and treachery will always defeat youth and bravado"

"There is no shame in appearing weak when you are in fact strong, but is essential to appear strong when you are in fact weak"

"When you are in a potentially dangerous situation try not to let your mind be polluted by emotions such as fear and anger"

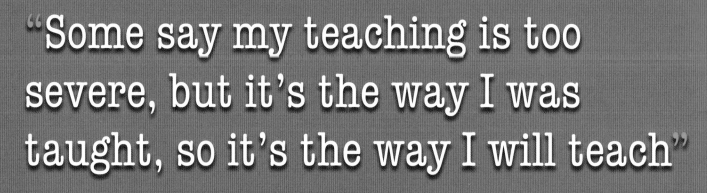

"Some say my teaching is too severe, but it's the way I was taught, so it's the way I will teach"

"If pushed, PULL.

"Confrontations are won with your brain not your brawn"

"Being prepared is not the same as being paranoid"

"In situations of danger it's sometimes better to REACT than think"

"Giving up can become habit forming"

"Whether you think you can or think you can't, you'll probably be right" if pulled, PUSH"

"You can run away or try harder the choice is always yours"

"You can develop the struggle you are having today into the strength you may need tomorrow"

"Self defence is protecting yourself. Protecting others is a trait of the warrior"

"Accept that fear is part of life, so stand tall and continue to move forward despite the throbbing in your head and the pounding in your heart that says.. Stay down, Stay down"

"You can't have discipline if you have no self-respect"

Stand in
to forge

the heart of nature and polish your edge

At home in the Derbyshire hills of the Peak District in the British Isles

Am I a warrior?
No
But I can fight and know the warriors traits
I can wield my weapon with malice and grace
I know where to strike him to break his resolve
And reduce him to nothing at a furious pace

So am I a warrior?
No
But I could heroically lead great armies
Or of course I could just be led
I could even lay down my life
And in the battles dust lie dead

So am I a warrior?
No
But I tread my own long and weary path
And I try so hard not to waver
I'm steadfast and strong and I think I'm brave
And I know how to stem my behaviour

So am I a warrior?
No
But I fight battles each and every day
I forge and test my beliefs and morals
I don't need to be the type that kills
But the type that appeases my quarrels

So am I a warrior?
Yes
Each road has battles a warrior must face
And it's fine to feel wrath towards those who would harm you
Whatever your role you're a warrior still
But you don't have to be the type that would kill

So are you a warrior?
Yes
You are a warrior my friend
Though sometimes in life we get it so wrong
And each life has its obstacles to overcome and conquer
It's the warrior inside that makes us resilient and strong

Poem by Steve Collins 2019

Personal Profile

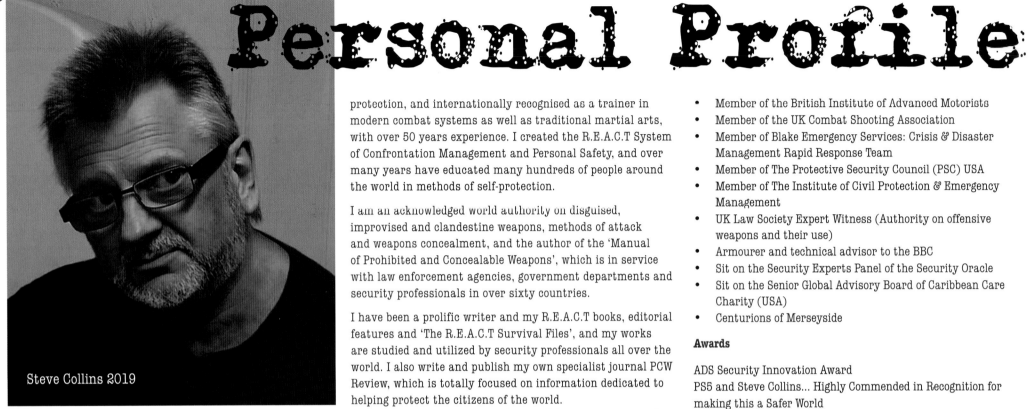

Steve Collins 2019

In 1986 I established my own business (PS5), which is now an internationally recognised specialist security consultancy, providing training and educational material to the law enforcement, defence and the security sectors.

The company's training wing 'R.E.A.C.T' delivers highly specialised training protocols to both the private and public sectors with specific focus on weapons related crime and personal protection from violence, aggressive behaviour and terrorism.

In order to carry out certain aspects of my company's highly sensitive work I hold a Home Office Authority approved by the Secretary of State under 'Section 5'. I have held this authority since 1993.

I have been an adviser to the US Department of Defence for the TSWG Mission for combating Terrorism.

I am considered an authority in close-quarter personal protection, and internationally recognised as a trainer in modern combat systems as well as traditional martial arts, with over 50 years experience. I created the R.E.A.C.T System of Confrontation Management and Personal Safety, and over many years have educated many hundreds of people around the world in methods of self-protection.

I am an acknowledged world authority on disguised, improvised and clandestine weapons, methods of attack and weapons concealment, and the author of the 'Manual of Prohibited and Concealable Weapons', which is in service with law enforcement agencies, government departments and security professionals in over sixty countries.

I have been a prolific writer and my R.E.A.C.T books, editorial features and 'The R.E.A.C.T Survival Files', and my works are studied and utilized by security professionals all over the world. I also write and publish my own specialist journal PCW Review, which is totally focused on information dedicated to helping protect the citizens of the world.

I now spend my time as a professional designer, writer and lecturer. I deliver training and interactive, discussion based lectures to government agencies, universities and corporate bodies on officer and public safety issues, with specific focus on weapons awareness and personal protection from violent attack.

Memberships and Affiliations

- Holder of a UK Government Secretary of State's authority under Section 5.
- Member of the Security Institute
- Member of IACSP (International Association of Counter-terrorism & Security Professionals)
- Member of the International Association of Security Drivers
- Member of the Chartered Institute of Journalists
- Member of A.D.S. (Aerospace Defence and Security)
- Member of ILEETA (International Law Enforcement Educators and Trainers Association)
- Member of the British Institute of Advanced Motorists
- Member of the UK Combat Shooting Association
- Member of Blake Emergency Services: Crisis & Disaster Management Rapid Response Team
- Member of The Protective Security Council (PSC) USA
- Member of The Institute of Civil Protection & Emergency Management
- UK Law Society Expert Witness (Authority on offensive weapons and their use)
- Armourer and technical advisor to the BBC
- Sit on the Security Experts Panel of the Security Oracle
- Sit on the Senior Global Advisory Board of Caribbean Care Charity (USA)
- Centurions of Merseyside

Awards

ADS Security Innovation Award
PS5 and Steve Collins... Highly Commended in Recognition for making this a Safer World

WINNER of the Skills for Security National Award for the most Innovative Security Training and Training Aid

NHS Award for Best Practice in the Preservation of Life

Dubai Police Academy
In recognition of helping to create safer communities in the UAE

Bravery Award
(carried an unconscious man out of a burning building)
The Society for the Protection of Life from Fire

Instructor Qualifications

- Master Instructor R.E.A.C.T
- Certified Close Protection & Security Planner
- Certified Close Quarter Combat Shooting Trainer
- Masters Degree - with the international Ki Do Association

- 5th Dan Black Belt-Korean Hapkido Close Quarter Combat Systems
- 3rd Dan Black Belt - AikiJutsu
- 3rd Dan Black Belt - Karate
- 2nd Dan Black Belt - Jujutsu
- Registered with the Association of Self Protection Instructors
- Master Instructor of the REACT-OR Compliance Tool
- Instructor to the International Law Enforcement Educators and Trainers Association
- Certified in Pressure Point Control Tactics PPCT (USA)
- Certified Skills for Security trainer in Weapons Awareness & Recognition
- Certified Skills for Security trainer in REACT Confrontation Management
- Close Quarter Concealed Firearms Tactics (Introduced and taught to UK Police forces and SO19 Royalty Protection Team by PS5)
- Lecturer in the history of personal protection at the University of Manchester

Creator of :
- The REACT System of Confrontation Management and Personal Safety
- PCW Review (Protecting Citizens Worldwide)
- The REACT Survival Files
- All REACT Tactical Solutions protocols and training manuals
- The REACT-OR compliance tool
- The ResQHook and Suite of products

PS5 Training Courses
- Weapons Awareness & Recognition
- Client Specific Weapons Awareness & Recognition
- I.E.D Recognition & Methods of Terrorist Attack
- Counter Terror & Security Search
- Rules for Dealing with an Armed Robbery
- Rules for Dealing with an Active Shooter
- Confrontation Management & Personal Protection
- We Go Prepared

Books, Feature Writing, Publications and Video Productions

Books - Authored
- The Manual of Prohibited and Concealable Weapons
- Think Safe, Act Safe, Stay Safe

- Avoiding and Surviving a Knife Attack
- Rules for Dealing with an Armed Robbery
- Rules for Dealing with Verbal & Physical Confrontation.
- Rules for Dealing with Age Related Sales
- Rules for Dealing with an Armed Robbery (Vehicles)
- Rules for Dealing with an Armed Robbery (Risk Managers)
- Rules for Dealing with Retail Crime.
- Rules for Dealing with the Active Shooter
- Rules for Dealing with Tiger Kidnap
- The R.E.A.C.T Survival Files

Books - Technical Adviser to:
- USA Department of Defence, Personnel Screening Guide (Restricted)
- Aviation Security (Challenges and Solutions)
- SAS Self Defence
- SAS Active Library Self Defence

New books - work in progress
- Junior REACT
- Women's REACT
- Verbal REACT
- Travel REACT
- Teacher's REACT

Publications produced and published
- PCW Review (Quarterly Journal)
- Total Control at Your Fingertips
- PCW BULLETIN

Training and Promotional Videos Produced and Directed
- Some Kind Of Gun
- Body Concealment and Search
- The ResQHook "The Knife that Saves Lives"
- Courtaulds Aerospace (Integrated Protection System)
- HIATTS. 'Speed-cuff' Training Video
- Kenyon. Temporary Mortuaries for Major Incidents
- Kenyon. International Emergency Services Video
- BCB. Personal Integrated Protection System (PIPS)
- ArmourShield (Ballistic Body Armour)
- Weapons Safety Bag (Ballistic Containment and Transportation)

Specialist Training Manuals produced
- R.E.A.C.T The System Master Trainers Manual

- REACT-OR Compliance Tool Manual Trainers Manual
- Counter Terrorist and Security Search Manual
- Counter Terrorist and Security Search
- Weapons Awareness and Recognition Trainers Manual

The Survival files published
- Stalking
- Bullying
- Stages of Violent Crime
- Car Jacking
- Family Violence
- Vehicle Security
- Travel Security
- At the Airport
- Kidnap
- Defence against Dogs
- Understanding Weapons
- Rape
- Spotting the Concealed Weapon
- The Non-metallic Threat
- Groping
- The Cycle of Behaviour
- Confrontation Management
- Faced with a Weapon
- Street Robbery
- Presumed Compliance
- Home Security
- Road Rage
- Sexual Offences
- The Intruder
- Anger
- Aftermath of an Armed Robbery
- REACT (A different way of thinking)

Editorial features
Written over 400 Editorial Features for international Security and Law Enforcement magazines and have a monthly column in 'Professional Security Magazine'

ResQHook (the knife that saves lives)
1988 - designed and manufactured the award winning ResQHook, which is now in service with Government bodies and rescue services around the world.

This profile is up to date - August 2019

Nobody is immune from falling victim to violent crime.

I have spent a lifetime developing training programmes to help people stay out of harm's way, and give them the tools to defend themselves.

Don't be one of those that buries their head in the sand, crosses their fingers and hopes it won't happen to them.

The following list shows the training courses that my company, PS5, delivers to both the private and public sectors worldwide

Confrontation Management & Personal Protection

REACT-OR
Compliance Tool

We Go Prepared
Living in an Age of Terrorism

Rules for Dealing with
an Armed Robbery

Rules for Dealing with
Tiger Kidnap

Weapons Awareness
& Recognition

I.E.D. Recognition &
Methods of Terrorist Attack

ETHOS
Specialist Training Protocols

Publishers
5T Publishing

Artwork
Mark Goodwin

Design & Art Direction
Steve Collins

Printed and bound in China 2019

This book was first created by
Steve Collins in 2019

First published 2019

©Copyright Steve Collins 2019

ISBN: 978-1-9161900-0-9

A catalogue record of this book is available from the British Library

I would like to thank the following people for their assistance in the creation of this publication :

Mark Goodwin

Terry Clayton

Darrell Johnson

Pierre Dalloz

Geoff Yeo

Brian Jenkins

Elaine Stranaghan

Elaine Musgrave

Mel Parry

Deborah Duckworth (dec.)

Of the many training courses my company has developed, the list below shows the programmes that are based around my R.E.A.C.T System

 Weapons Awareness & Recognition

 I.E.D. Recognition & Methods of Terrorist Attack

 We Go Prepared

 Rules for Dealing with an Armed Robbery

 Confrontation Management & Personal Protection

 REACT-OR Compliance Tool

 ETHOS Specialist Training Protocols

For more information about Steve Collins's Training and Educational Programmes please contact him at:
steve@ps5.com or info@5Tpublishing.com
PS5
Nemus House
32 London Road
Hazel Grove
Cheshire
SK7 4AH
UK
+44(0)161 482 7800

"Over 60 years of training, teaching, designing and writing have culminated in this slim volume.

Six decades is a long time to do anything, but I still love it as much now as I did when I started.

What keeps my passion warm, you might ask?

Well in the words of Michelangelo...

"Indignation, best fuel I know... it never burns out.""